D1095766

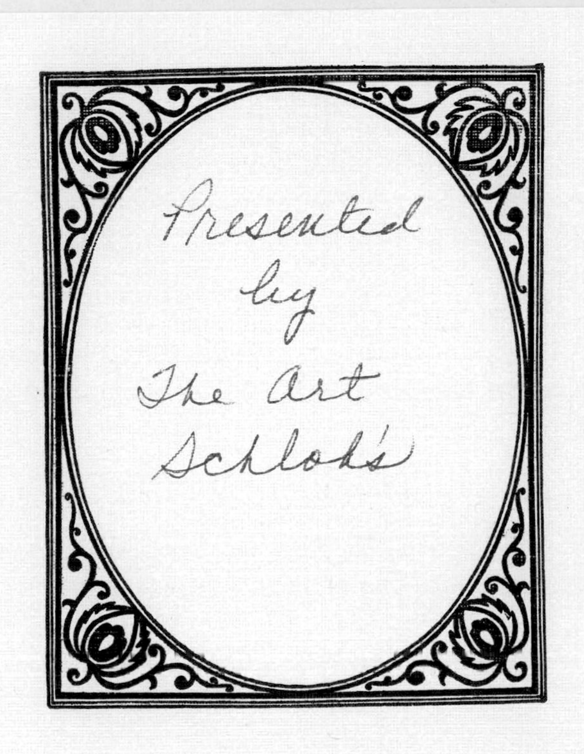
Presented
by
The Art
Schlok's

PERSONALITIES AROUND JESUS

Also by William P. Barker

TWELVE WHO WERE CHOSEN
SAINTS IN APRONS AND OVERALLS
KINGS IN SHIRTSLEEVES

PERSONALITIES AROUND JESUS

William P. Barker

FLEMING H. REVELL  COMPANY

Acknowledgment is made to The Macmillan Company for permission to reprint lines from "The Everlasting Mercy" (*Poems*), by John Masefield, © 1935.

Unless otherwise indicated, the Scripture passages in this book are from the *Revised Standard Version of the Bible*, copyrighted 1946 and 1952.

 WESTWOOD, NEW JERSEY • LIBRARY OF CONGRESS CATALOG CARD NUMBER: 63-17108 • PRINTED IN THE UNITED STATES OF AMERICA • 1.2

TO *PEG* AND *LEE,*
MAY AND *ELMORE,*
SHIRLEY AND *JARVIS*

A special note of thanks

To Mrs. Howard E. Betts and Mrs. Fred F. Smoot for typing and proofreading—

To John B. Barker, James G. Gardner, Frank S. Mead, and Fred M. Rogers for suggestions and criticisms—

To Jean, Jock, and Ellen for their interest and encouragement.

CONTENTS

PERSONALITIES AROUND JESUS

I

Mary, the Mother of Jesus

IN CUSHING, Oklahoma, a few years ago, an elderly recluse named George Williams was found dead. The coroner reported that the old man died of starvation. On his body, however, the police had found over ten thousand dollars in cash.

This is somewhat the situation we Christians are in. We have clung to the gospel but we have never quite known what to do about it. Desperately in need of help, we have never quite understood what the Good News means. We have carried around the riches of the life, death, and resurrection of Jesus Christ for years.

One way to understand afresh the significance of Jesus Christ in our lives is to know the personalities around Jesus. These people—so startlingly like us—were the people He talked to, the people He transformed. Seeing Jesus through their eyes gives us new insight into the meaning of this God-Man of Nazareth.

We can most easily start with the person who knew Him first—Mary, His mother.

It is not surprising that a woman was the first person at Jesus' cradle, and that women were the last to linger at His cross. They had never known a man like this Man.

Mary, the mother of Jesus, is first mentioned in the Bible as a girl, probably in her teens. She was engaged. Marriage is entered early in the East, so Mary's age was probably what we would call "high-school age." She undoubtedly came from a peasant home and was used to hard rounds of daily toil.

Both Mary and her betrothed Joseph were devout Jews. They had observed the usual religious customs of the time when they became engaged. Pious Jewish couples always allowed an interval of a year to elapse between the times of their engagement and their wedding. This sort of intermediary time between engagement and marriage was called "betrothal." Although betrothed couples did not live together, they were legally bound to one another.

Life changed suddenly and drastically for the young peasant girl. A messenger appeared to her with an astounding announcement: she was to become God's instrument by giving birth to a Baby who would be God's anointed.

The message was unnerving. Mary trusted God enough to be His agent for this amazing plan; at the same time, she was uneasy. Pregnant, and not married? What would others say? Tongues would wag, especially in a small, strait-laced place like Nazareth (which had its own synagogue and was considered very religious).

More important, what would Joseph say? Would he believe her? Would he call things off, then and there?

There were certainly barbed comments and lewd leers. Mary tried to keep going with her trust in God, but it was lonely to be so different. She knew she was "the handmaid of the Lord" (Luke 1:38), but it was hard to stay in town. Trembling with hope and fright and embarrassment, she finally went up to the hill country to be with her cousin Elizabeth. With Elizabeth, she was away from the smirks and gossip, and had the comfort of someone who understood. Perhaps Mary's own mother was dead. In any case, Elizabeth gave Mary the mothering she needed.

Joseph agreed to go through with his original plans, and he married Mary. Then a high-handed bureaucratic decree forced the young couple to make an exhausting, three-day journey to Bethlehem to register and pay taxes. Mary was tired physically and emotionally by the time they reached Bethlehem. Knowing she was so near her time of delivery, she must have desperately hoped that she would not go into labor along the road, where she was without shelter or help.

Pain and poverty were grim realities throughout Mary's life. A hewn-out cave in a limestone cliff, used usually to shelter animals, was the only place she and Joseph could locate in crowded Bethlehem. That night, she delivered her own child and named Him Jesus.

Did she have her moments of doubt? God had told her she was to bring forth "a king." Yet she and her baby were in a dark, smelly cavern not even used by human beings.

Then some shepherds came to look at her Baby. They had strange words of praise; it was very perplexing. Mary "kept all these things, pondering them in her heart" (Luke 2:19).

Mary's troubles were only beginning. Rumors of her Son's birth had reached Herod, the mad tyrant who had life-or-death powers over the people. Herod ruthlessly ordered the slaughter of all male infants in Bethlehem to prevent anyone from becoming a "king." Terror-stricken, Mary and Joseph took their Child and slipped away to the south and safety.

Providentially, Herod died shortly after, and the couple came home. In keeping with Jewish practice, Mary stopped in Jerusalem at the Temple to offer prayers of thanks after childbirth. The usual gift was a lamb. In the case of poverty, a pair of doves was sufficient. Mary could only afford the doves.

The Boy Jesus grew. To Mary, He was perplexing. For example, there was the time they took Him to Jerusalem for His confirmation when He was about twelve. Traveling home, the men usually went in one group, the women in another, and it was a couple of days before Mary and Joseph discovered that Jesus was not with either group. Returning to Jerusalem, they found Him in the Temple talking with the teachers. Mary was put out: "Son, why have you treated us so?" (Luke 2:48). His answer blew away her annoyance: "Did you not know that I must be in my Father's house?" (v. 49). These serious words came from a twelve-year-old.

Nothing more is said of Mary in the Bible for what would have been a period of about eighteen years. They must have been hard years that only a mother could understand: long hours cooking, mending, cleaning; children to feed, comfort, discipline, nurse; a meager budget, especially if Joseph had died, leaving her with five sons and at least two daughters to look after. Mary must have known bone-deep weariness; she must have noticed the stooped shoulders and thickening waist that the years and toil were producing. She must have continued to wonder about those things that had taken place at Jesus' birth.

The next Biblical reference to Mary shows her upset and pushing Jesus to do something. She is in charge of a wedding reception at nearby Cana. A crisis has occurred: the wine has given out. This is an unspeakable lack of hospitality and could mean a disgrace for life for the newlyweds. Jumpy and nervous, Mary turns to Jesus and prods Him to do something. Jesus smilingly calms His mother and quietly saves the day.

Soon Jesus is becoming something of a well-known Person. He is busy healing and preaching, and people are beginning to talk about His claims. There are rumors that some are out to "get" Him. Mary shows herself to be a possessive mother on one occasion and tries to interfere with what He is doing. When she comes to the edge of a crowd around Him and sends word that she wants to bring Him home, Jesus sweeps His hand over the crowd and announces that anyone who does the will of God is really His mother and brother and sister.

This painful scene reveals that poor Mary really did not fully understand Jesus or His mission at that time. She wanted Him to have a crown, not a cross. She could not comprehend the meaning of His approaching sacrifice and disgrace.

However, she faithfully followed her Son to Jerusalem and was one of the pitifully small cluster of friends who actually saw him die. It was a ghastly sight, even for anyone who did not know the victim, a sight few of us could have stomached. Mary not only stood by but was aware that the Condemned was her own Son.

From her moments of misunderstanding and shame at the time of His birth to the misunderstanding and shame surrounding His death, Mary had taken it all. Mary and John, the disciple closest to Jesus, stood at the cross. Almost in His last breath, Jesus told them that each was to be the special care of the other. "Woman, behold thy son!" (John 19:26, KJV), He told Mary, indicating that John was to be her special care. In turn, John was told that Mary was to be his special care. Mary then made her home with John.

Many others stopped believing in Jesus after the crucifixion; Mary did not. The last reference to her in the New Testament is in connection with the birth of the Christian church. About one hundred and twenty believers were gathered for prayer, when the Holy Spirit came among them. Among those present, according to Acts 1:14, was "Mary, the mother of Jesus" (KJV).

From there, she drops from sight. We read no more about the nobody named Mary who, as the wife of Joseph and the mother of Jesus, was a somebody to God. Thus we honor the peasant girl of Nazareth, and we worship her Son as Saviour.

It is interesting that the last reference to Mary in the New Testament shows that she was an active participant in the young Christian church. She was another humble member, not a supernatural "Mother of God" claiming pre-eminence because of her kinship to Jesus.

Mary's story reminds us of how unpredictable God is and how dependable God is. Contradictory? Not a bit. God is unpredictable. He picked out Mary to bring Jesus into the world. God chose not a woman with royal name, fame, or background, but an unknown, a nobody. Mary had no education, wealth, advantageous marriage, or special qualities marking her as unusually gifted. So little is said about her in the Bible that we can almost conclude she was rather unobtrusive. How unpredictable of God to select such a person as Mary to be His agent.

You with your sense of inferiority may bemoan your lack of education, your mediocre abilities. You may be embarrassed by your commonplace job, and resent the drudgery of your daily routine. You may be resigned to being an anonymous blob with a mop. But our God does the unpredictable. He seems to prefer the simple, the ordinary, the commonplace. Unpredictably, He chooses Mary and you and me to serve Him and continue His work.

At the same time, our God is dependable. We are all conscious of our own frailties and weaknesses. As mothers or fathers, we are often ready to abdicate. How could God want us to undertake such an awesome task? Just as Mary pondered these things in her heart, so we are perplexed and wondering about the complex personalities of our own offspring. Flesh of our flesh and blood, and yet our own children often seem as strangers. Just as Mary once fretted, "He is beside himself" (Mark 3:21, KJV), so we fuss at our children. They are never always the way we want them to be.

Our God is dependable. He is with us. He completes what we work at. The housewife married to Joseph of Nazareth learned that. So must we all.

2

Philip

MANY OF us have the idea that the Twelve Jesus chose were supersaints. These disciples have been so covered with the varnish of sanctity that it is hard to realize they were actually weak, mortal men.

"Paint me," Oliver Cromwell insisted, "warts and all!" A portrait of any of the Twelve Apostles, painted "warts and all," reveals a personality astoundingly similar to any of us!

Philip is a good case in point. Dull, unimaginative, and hesitant, Philip embodies all the least attractive characteristics of the Christian church. An ancient chronicler, Clement of Alexandria, recorded a tradition that Philip was the anonymous man who was called by Jesus and who begged off, asking that he first be allowed to bury his father (Matthew 8:21). The nameless, would-be disciple was preoccupied with custom and trivia, unable to see that following Jesus meant a radical new way of living.

Whether or not the man was Philip, we have no way of knowing. We do know, however, that Philip was from Bethsaida, the hometown of Peter and Andrew. Bethsaida was the fishermen's quarter on the north shore of Galilee. Undoubtedly Philip, like many other disciples, was also a burly fisherman.

Jesus "found" Philip, as the Gospel of John puts it, suggesting that Philip had previously been "lost." Found by Jesus, Philip in turn found himself to be a different person.

Philip immediately "found" Nathanael. Surprising himself with his enthusiasm and eloquence, Philip beat his friend's ear with an electrifying speech: "We have found him, of whom Moses in the law, and also the prophets, did write, Jesus of Nazareth, the son of Joseph" (John 1:45, KJV).

Nathanael was unimpressed. He growled, "Can anything good come out of Nazareth?" (v. 46). Wisely, Philip simply answered, "Come and see!"

Theological debate has its place, but it misses the point if it fails to urge others to come and see Jesus Christ. No one was ever argued into the Kingdom. Jesus calls us not to dispute but to invite. "Come and see" is still the best retort to any skeptic.

In spite of his commitment to Jesus, in spite of his invitation to Nathanael, in spite of his call to be one of the Twelve, Philip was a run-of-the-mill person. His appearances in the New Testament are all in John's gospel, almost as if John were trying to rescue Philip from complete oblivion. Moreover, John's portrait of Philip shows plenty of warts.

Take the scene of the feeding of the five thousand. Philip saw only the problems. There were a hundred and one reasons why nothing could be done for the crowds, Philip knew. Multiplying the cost of a snack at so much per head by the estimated five thousand people present, Philip found it came to big money. Then he divided the meager disciple treasury by five thousand, but he found that it would go far enough. Philip had the mathematical view of life, and thought he could handle every problem with a slide rule and a cash register.

Philip's big mistake was in trying to reckon without Jesus; he did his figuring without Jesus' power. Philip's mind that day was like a child's bank: nothing but nickels and dimes could go in or out of it.

When a lad stepped forth to offer his lunch of a few loaves and fishes, Philip pooh-poohed the idea. Unimaginative Philip could see no use for so little when there was need for so much. Common sense is a virtue, but with Philip it had become an obsession. He never dreamed what Jesus could do with one boy's lunch.

Miracles still happen with Jesus and little boys' gifts. A couple of years ago, a thirteen-year-old Negro boy named Robert Hill, son of a United States Army sergeant stationed in Italy, read of Albert Schweitzer. Robert Hill was deeply impressed with Dr. Schweitzer's ministry of healing for Jesus Christ in steaming Africa, and decided to contribute a bottle of aspirin. He asked the Allied Air Force Commander in Southern Europe if an Air Force plane could drop the aspirin bottle at Albert Schweitzer's hospital.

Somehow, an Italian radio station picked up the story. Many laughed at it. To everyone's surprise, however, other medical supplies began to flow in. A few weeks later, four and one-half tons of medicines and equipment worth over $400,000 had been collected. Planes provided by the French and Italian governments flew Robert Hill and the medical supplies to Dr. Schweitzer's hospital. Dr. Schweitzer said, "I never thought a child could do so much for my hospital."

Philip was dumbfounded when Jesus took the lad's loaves and fishes and fed the multitude. He thought, "I never thought a child could do so much." What can faith and five loaves do? Philip had asked himself.

"What can faith and five dollars do?" people asked when a Presbyterian minister's widow, Louise Wotring Lyle, proposed to help the needy and sick of Pittsburgh. Mrs. Lyle had only her trust in Jesus Christ and her five dollars, but in 1893 she rented half of a double house on Sherman Avenue, on Pittsburgh's north side, and launched a hospital. She was ignored at first, then criticized by many leading churchmen. There was even a hassle over her naming the hospital, "The Presbyterian Hospital." Some thought it degraded Presbyterianism! Louise Lyle was concerned only that the poor of Pittsburgh should have adequate care in time of illness.

Thanks to Louise Lyle's "five dollars and faith in Almighty God," Presbyterian-University Hospital and Nursing School today is the leading surgical and medical unit of the Medical Center hospitals in Pittsburgh.

Philip lacked the imagination of the boy with the five loaves, and the imaginations of Robert Hill and Louise Lyle. He was "practical," "reasonable," "sensible."

Imagination is the research department of the soul. Without imagination, our faith will never do very much. Our commitment to Jesus Christ becomes adventurous only when we allow Him to take over our imaginations. When our imaginations, as well as our minds, are converted God gives wings to our creativity.

Philip was unimaginative on another occasion when some "Greeks" asked to meet Jesus. Whether these Greeks were government officials or curious tourists or interested visitors, we are not sure. Philip, the disciple with the Greek name (meaning "lover of horses"), was the person the Greeks approached. "Sir," they asked Philip, "we wish to see Jesus" (John 12:21).

Cautious by nature, Philip was reluctant to try something new. No one else had ever brought outsiders to Jesus. Philip was not sure that he wanted to stick his neck out. He played it safe; he turned the people over to Andrew.

The janitor of a church, when asked why he got on so well with everyone, answered, "Well, I just throw my mind into neutral and go where I'm pushed." This could be the motto for timid, cautious discipleship.

Jesus' ministry had a reckless courage about it. He meant to infect men with the same vision, the same Self-abandon that He had. Philip could not stretch his thinking to understand that Jesus cared about Greeks as much as He cared about Jews. Lacking a vision of the grand strategy of God in Jesus Christ, Philip could only mumble excuses and walk away.

God came in Jesus Christ to all men. He declared His intentions to mankind in the birth, life, death, and resurrection of Jesus. In Jesus Christ, the master plan of the Almighty was expressed.

Only a few, however, have begun to understand the vastness of God's mighty act in Jesus Christ, and to mold their strategies accordingly. Paul was one. ". . . from Jerusalem and as far round as Illyricum I have fully preached the gospel of Christ . . ." he wrote (Romans 15:19). From the boundaries of the East to the boundaries of the West, Paul envisioned the rule of Christ.

"Give me all of Scotland ere I die," cried John Knox, aflame with the gospel. He was another who knew that the gospel was for all people. Still another who had this vision and regulated his thinking in large terms was pioneer-missionary Sheldon Jackson. Walking, snow-shoeing, dog-sledding throughout the western territories and Alaska to organize churches, Jackson was dubbed "bishop of all beyond."

Poor Philip lacked such vision. We might excuse him for not evangelizing distant provinces, but we can hardly condone his reluctance to introduce some people to his Master. Philip took a long time to realize that discipleship often means going out on a limb for others. It wasn't until he saw his Lord on a limb for him, nailed and dying, that Philip understood the price of following Jesus.

A Christian must expect to go out on a limb for others. William Wilberforce, a devout Christian, was the first to go out on a limb to oppose slavery in the British Empire. He was vilified by the press, scorned by associates. Experts testified that Wilberforce's schemes to end slavery would ruin the economy of the country. Whenever Wilberforce arose to speak in Parliament, his subject was the evils of slavery. Dozens always got up and walked out; fellow members of Commons called him "the most tiresome member of Parliament." Wilberforce was snubbed, reviled, and left with little reputation, but in 1833, just before he died, he saw the passage of a bill that ended slavery in all British possessions.

A Christian is a marked person. But so was Jesus; He was marked literally—with nails. Jesus tried to make it plain to the Twelve that He would suffer such marks. The disciples, however, were incredibly slow to understand Him. Jesus also tried to help His disciples to realize that He and the Father were one. Again, the Twelve were annoyingly dull.

The best example of this was at the Last Supper—a heartbreak for Jesus. The Twelve proved to be a real disappointment. To begin with, each childishly refused to perform the lackey's chore of washing the others' feet. When Jesus arrived, He found them sitting in sullen silence and shocked them out of their mood by picking up the basin and towel and doing what they had been too proud to do.

The conversation touched on many topics around that table: Judas' betrayal, Peter's denial, the new commandment to love one another. Throughout the evening, Jesus spoke again and again of His approaching death. Knowing how the disciples would go to pieces when He was crucified, Jesus tried to prepare them: "Let not your hearts be troubled; believe in God, believe also in me. In my Father's house are many rooms . . . ," Jesus explained (John 14:1-2). "I go to prepare a place for you."

Thomas interrupted to ask where Jesus was going, and the way. Jesus carefully answered, "I am the way, and the truth, and the life; no one comes to the Father, but by me. If you had known me, you would have known my Father also; henceforth you know him and have seen him" (v. 6).

What clearer statement of Jesus' divinity could anyone want? What more precise and concise description of Jesus' relationship to the Father could be made?

Philip, however, was still not quite certain; everything had to be in black and white for him. After the magnificent disclosure by Jesus, following Thomas' question, and at a time when any further questions or remarks were out of place, Philip piped up. His question was as much an anticlimax to Jesus' remarks as a penny whistle solo after a symphony. "Lord," said Philip, "show us the Father, and we shall be satisfied" (v. 8).

Jesus' irritation shone through His answer: "Have I been with you so long, and yet you do not know me, Philip? He who has seen me has seen the Father; how can you say, 'Show us the Father'?" (v. 9).

When Philip said, "Show us the Father," he spoke *the* question of life; it is still being asked. Philip spoke for all of us. Recently, for example, beatnik Jack Kerouac told a newsman, "I want God to show me His face."

Jesus spells it out in A-B-C terms that *anyone* can understand: "He who has seen me has seen the Father." Jesus answers the question, "What is God like?" for all time.

Most of us have a peculiar mental picture of God as a huge, mean ogre, and another mental picture of Jesus as a smiling, friendly-looking midget standing beside the ogre. Some almost hint that Jesus is a sort of ventriloquist's dummy, pleasant and helpless, perched on the lap of a great, cruel giant named "God." We may be attracted to the winsome Jesus, but we fear that suspicious, frightening unknown Being behind Him.

Through Jesus, the Father identified with us. God stepped down onto the stage of space and time in the Person of Jesus Christ. The Inexpressible chose to express Himself in the life, death, and resurrection of Jesus; the Invisible became visible.

"Have I been with you so long, and yet you do not know me, Philip?" No, Philip had not known Jesus. Nor have we understood Jesus. We think we have, but one look at our tame, innocuous "Christianity" makes it obvious that we have not known Christ. We have not recognized Him for the God and Saviour He really is.

One time after the War Between the States, Robert E. Lee and his daughter Mildred were horseback-riding in the Blue Ridge Mountains when a sudden, violent thunder shower overtook them. Soaking wet, they galloped to a cabin nearby. Lee lifted his daughter off her horse and rushed her into the cabin, then led the horses to a shed. When General Lee reappeared in the cabin, the atmosphere was uncomfortable. The reticent mountain woman who lived there was not pleased that a strange woman had come dripping into her spotless cabin. Still less did she relish the arrival of the booted man, tramping mud and leaving pools of water wherever he paused on the boards she had so laboriously scoured white. Lee sensed her indignation, and in the same breath in which he asked for permission to remain until the rain stopped, he apologized for marring the beauty of her floor. Somewhat mollified, she grudgingly permitted the visitors to remain.

The walls of the cabin were adorned with pictures of Robert E. Lee in full uniform, but the woman never associated the man before her with the soldier. After a while, the rain subsided, and Lee with impeccable courtesy thanked the woman profusely for her hospitality. Lee's daughter Mildred paused after her father had gone for the horses and obligingly told her hostess who her visitor was. The mountain woman was stunned at the incredible news that her hero had been under her roof without her knowing it.

We think we know Jesus. Our tributes and creeds and doctrines about Jesus are hanging everywhere. We adorn our faith with pretty talk about Him as "Saviour," "Lord," "Master." The real Person of Jesus Christ, however, is a Stranger, someone we do not really know.

God actually stood among us briefly in human form. We became annoyed because He got in the way, upset our plans, and caused so much inconvenience; we pushed Him out the back door of life by crucifying Him. Most amazing, we still have not begun to realize that Jesus Christ is *God*, right here in the main room of our existence!

Philip was one of the least gifted, least colorful of the Twelve. Some others had flashes of greatness, but not Philip. Peter preached, John healed, Matthew wrote, but Philip was more like most of us.

There is a place for the Philips in the church. Much as we need brains in the church, much as God uses thinkers, writers, theologians, artists, and other creative minds to interpret His eternal promise to our times, He also uses Philips. We do not have to show a Ph. D. to be a Christian. God calls the slow and prosaic—like Philip and like many of us—to the disciple band.

We are told by the author of Acts that Philip was one of those who assembled in the upper room after the resurrection. Years later, Polycrates, the great Bishop of Ephesus in the latter part of the second century, wrote that Philip, "one of the Twelve," was "one of the great lights of Asia" and that he was buried at Hierapolis.

There are various traditions about Philip's subsequent career. Some recount that he traveled and preached in various parts of Greece and Asia Minor. Many stories indicate that he was martyred, claiming that he was stoned first, then crucified head downward. Apart from the Bible, the most definite evidence about Philip's life is an ancient inscription that archaeologists unearthed in the ruins of a building in Hierapolis, stating that the building is the church of "Philip the Apostle."

Hans Clous in *Conversation With the Earth* writes, "I knew geology second-hand from books, but at age twenty-four became a geologist forever by seeing with my own eyes Vesuvius in eruption. I cried, 'The earth is alive!' "

Philip had known God second-hand. He became a believer forever by seeing with his own eyes the Almighty in human form, suffering and dying, and risen and living. He then knew that God is alive!

3

Andrew

THE LATE Bishop Francis McConnell had a younger brother Pat who was also a Methodist minister. Less renowned than his famous bishop-brother, Pat McConnell used to laugh and say that he went through life as the victim of the "double handshake." Whenever he was introduced to a stranger, he would receive the normal, perfunctory greeting. Most certainly, then, someone would mention that Pat McConnell was the brother of the well-known bishop. The stranger would invariably brighten, stride back to Pat, grab his hand a second time, and shake it much more heartily than he had at first.

Andrew was also a victim of the "double handshake." Brother of Simon Peter, Andrew was eclipsed by his illustrious relative. Peter was the gifted orator, the born leader. Peter became famous and made the headlines. Comparing ordinary Andrew to the flamboyant Peter is like contrasting a streetlight to a skyrocket.

Andrew was willing to be overshadowed by Peter, and did not object that his brother was in the spotlight. Andrew was willing to play "second fiddle" all his life.

Nobody really likes being the second fiddle. Yet, much of the time, we must be just that. Most Americans work for others, many in large corporations where there is a carefully structured hierarchy of jobs. Inevitably, a great many of us, capable men and women, are going to have to play second fiddle much of our working lives. Most of us are going to be overshadowed by someone higher up.

When we are eclipsed by another, even the best of us may become jealous. An ancient fable from the early church in North Africa relates that the devil came across a group of lesser fiends trying to tempt a godly church father who was praying alone in the desert. The minor devils had tried unsuccessfully to divert the holy man with pleasant fleshly temptations. They had tried to work on the man's doubts and fears, but he withstood their attempts to undermine his faith.

The devil, according to the old tale, haughtily stepped forward and informed the junior tempters that their methods were crude. Addressing the devout old hermit, who had withstood all the wiles of the other evil powers, the devil said, "Have you heard the news? Your brother has just been made bishop of Alexandria!" With that, the serene face of the venerable holy man was clouded by a scowl of jealousy.

Remarkably, Andrew never acted jealously of his more-famous brother.

Playing second fiddle can also produce despair. Our culture dictates that every man must become a president, a chief, a major-domo, a head man of some sort. Otherwise, he is dubbed a "failure," a nonentity. The person playing second fiddle, we have been led to think, is not a "success."

No one bothers to mention that there is room for only a handful of "big men." Most of us, like it or not, are going to be second fiddles because there is not enough room at the top.

The Horatio Alger rules of hard work, frugality, and a big smile do not mean that we inevitably end up at the top of the ladder. Many who followed the Horatio Alger advice find themselves still on the lower rungs at age fifty-five or sixty. More than one man has a deep sense of uneasiness over being a second fiddle; he feels guilty for "not working hard enough," "not succeeding."

More than one woman despairs over being overshadowed by others. Marriage for most women means putting a husband and children into prominence. Most wives and mothers automatically disqualify themselves from being a first fiddle. Only such a woman knows how much of her status, her freedom, her comforts, and her interests she has sacrificed for her family. Playing second fiddle seems to give some women a stigma. Too often, when a woman replies that she is "only a housewife," one has the feeling that she is really saying, "I haven't amounted to much, have I?"

Andrew never was bothered by the fact that he was relegated to a minor role. He never despaired because he did not win the applause and honors that Peter his brother received.

Success or failure does not depend on whether or not we are first fiddles. Second fiddle or first—it really does not matter which we play, as long as we play in response to the call of Jesus Christ.

Andrew's entire career was a response to Jesus. As a young man, Andrew had been deeply stirred by the revival movement of John the Baptist. One day, John pointed out Jesus, indicating that Jesus was greater than he or any other prophet. Andrew promptly stepped up to Jesus. All afternoon and until late that night, Andrew and Jesus talked. After that, Andrew was Jesus' man through and through.

Unlike his brother Peter, who once jumped into the sea for Jesus, Andrew was not given to impulse. Nor did he make heady promises, such as "Though they all fall away . . . , I will never . . ." (Matthew 26:33). Andrew did not go in for the bravado of Peter, who dramatically hacked off a servant's ear to show his loyalty to Jesus. A quiet, firm man of decision, Andrew also seems colorless and dull. Andrew, nonetheless, is the disciple who had the courage to be first.

Andrew was the first follower of Jesus Christ, the first of the Twelve to be chosen. It took courage to be the first follower. Jesus was a Carpenter from up in the hills at Nazareth. "Can there any good thing come out of Nazareth?" (John 1:46, KJV), people in those days joked. To be the first follower of the Carpenter-turned-Teacher took a special kind of courage.

Andrew knew he would be laughed at. He was a Galilean fisherman, and he knew the rough humor of his fishermen-buddies. Why should he break with tradition? Why get mixed up with a cause nobody knew anything about? Why be out of step, why face ridicule and criticism for responding to the call of a young unknown Rabbi, Jesus? Surely these thoughts crossed Andrew's mind. In spite of his own misgivings or his friends' criticisms, Andrew had the courage to become the first disciple.

Andrew's life as a Christian was full of "first's." He was also the first home missionary. The first thing Andrew did after meeting Jesus Christ was to hunt up his brother Peter and introduce him to Jesus. Andrew saw that discipleship started with those nearest. A man of few words or flowery phrases, Andrew came right to the point with Peter. "We," he said, "have found the Messiah" (John 1:41).

These words say a lot about Andrew. "We" means that he understood that Jesus was not just Andrew's private chaplain, but everyone's Master. "We" also means that Andrew was convinced that Jesus was the One whom Peter needed and was seeking.

Notice also that Andrew bluntly stated that Jesus was the Messiah. Saying this claim aloud was like detonating a charge of TNT. Andrew, however, did not equivocate or back down. Jesus, he was certain, *was* the Messiah, and not another rabbi, prophet, or what-have-you. Jesus was the Messiah, and the good news had to be told to Peter.

It took a rare type of courage to be the first home missionary. It takes a rare courage to be a witness for Jesus Christ in our own neighborhoods even now. A Christian housewife in a small town in California was such a witness recently. A young Negro got a job in a neighborhood gas station to earn his way through teachers' college. Some of the customers at the gas station objected, saying they did not want to buy their gas from a Negro. The uneasy owner was about to fire the student when the housewife asked, "How many customers will you lose?"

"About eighteen or twenty."

"If I get you twenty new customers, will you keep him on?"

"You bet I will!"

So the woman got twenty new customers and five more for good measure. She was a housewife, but she spoke and acted in concern for that young student. She had the courage to witness for Jesus Christ in her own neighborhood.

Andrew also had the courage to be the first Christian social worker. Five thousand people had walked out to spend a day listening to Jesus. By late afternoon, they were tired and hungry. Nobody volunteered to help feed the masses except a small boy with five loaves and two fishes. Everybody dismissed the boy's offer as impractical; some even regarded the boy as a nuisance. Only Andrew listened to the lad's offer, accepted the lunch, and took it to Jesus.

Andrew was courageous enough to be the first disciple to care about people and their human needs. He was concerned about others because he had grown to know that Jesus was concerned. Caring about the needs of others demanded a tenacious kind of courage.

As recently as 1910, two million children from the ages of ten to fifteen worked full time in factories and mines.

The working hours were cruelly long, but the owners and operators of industries that hired children vigorously resisted changing their policies. Many justified child labor on the grounds that it kept children off the streets.

A man named Charles Loring Brace had the courage to be the first to protest the practice of child labor. Concerned about the welfare of millions of working youngsters, he pressed for legislation to prevent the horrible abuses then prevalent. For his pains, he was dubbed an "officious fool" in Parliament and a "meddler" in American legislatures.

No laws were necessary, the powerful interests shrilled. As one mill owner in Georgia put it, the owners were already being more than generous: they were voluntarily limiting the working hours of ten-year-olds to sixty-six hours per week!

Charles Loring Brace founded the Children's Aid Society, which became the Society for the Prevention of Cruelty to Children. The first to campaign and organize to abolish child exploitation, Brace was a man of rare courage.

It seems that nearly every time Andrew appears in the New Testament he was bringing somebody to Jesus! First it was his brother; next it was a boy. Andrew did not need a crowd or an audience. Quietly, effectively, he took the good news of Jesus, his Messiah, to individuals.

Andrew was even willing to let the bars down and take the good news to outsiders. He had the courage to be the first foreign missionary. He took care of the "Greeks" who asked to meet Jesus. These "Greeks" were actually Greek-speaking Jews, descendants of Jews who had emigrated from Palestine. To the strict Jews in Palestine, these people were "foreigners."

The disciples of Jesus also looked down on Greek-speaking Jews as strangers and outsiders. Shying away from taking them to Jesus, several of the disciples discussed the problem among themselves. It was Andrew who was willing to break with tradition. Courageously, he introduced the "Greeks" to the Master.

Andrew was the first to see that the gospel was for all men and women, and he was willing to back his conviction with action. It takes courage to be the first to take the good news of Jesus Christ to people who are "different."

William Carey was a young shoemaker in England. Over his cobbler's bench hung a map of the world that he had made himself. Beside him, as he worked, were books. From these books he taught himself to read and write. The young cobbler even taught himself languages. He mastered French and Dutch, then Latin, Greek, and Hebrew. Meanwhile, he was also studying his Bible.

William Carey was convinced that those in foreign countries should hear the good news of Jesus Christ. This penniless cobbler was the first to suggest sending Christian missionaries to other parts of the world.

When Carey first brought up his concern for people in foreign lands at a church meeting, he was hooted down. His idea was ridiculed and opposed by everyone present. "Young man," one leading member rebuked, "when God intends to save heathen, He will do it without your help or mine."

Carey had the courage to keep pleading in other meetings. Insisting that it was the duty of the church to send missionaries, the poverty-stricken shoemaker devised ways to go himself to India.

The powerful East India Company refused him passage. In the words of one company official, "The sending out of missionaries into our Eastern possession is the maddest, most extravagant, most costly, most indefensible project which has ever been suggested by a moonstruck fanatic. Such a scheme is pernicious, impudent, useless, harmful, dangerous, profitless, fantastic."

After ten years of trying, William Carey finally arrived

in India in 1793. Truly the father of the modern mission movement, Carey had the courage to be first.

It is not easy to stand up for Jesus Christ among strangers—or for strangers. We need more Andrews who will remember that outsiders are people too—God's people. Our world cries out for more courageous people who will bring those who are "different from us" to Jesus Christ. The color of a man's skin, the place where he was born, the sound of his accent—these do not matter with Him who has come in Jesus Christ, reconciling *all* men to Himself.

Andrew's name, a Greek name, means literally "brave" or "manly." He lived a brave, manly life. We hear far more about his famous brother, yet Andrew had a key part to play in the economy of God. Where would Peter have been, had it not been for Andrew?

Where would so many of the world's "greats" be, were it not for the Andrews? It takes exceptional courage to be willing to be little so that somebody else can be big!

The list of the Twelve Disciples varies somewhat in the various gospel accounts because some disciples were known by different names and certain ones were better known than others. Significantly, however, Andrew's name is always on the list of the Twelve in every gospel. Even more significantly, Andrew's name is always among the first four names listed!

Andrew lived a life of courage, and died the same way. Tradition insists that he died in Patrae in Achaia on a cross. That cross, at Andrew's insistence, was shaped like the letter "X." Andrew claimed that he was not worthy to die on a cross shaped like the one on which Jesus had died.

To this day, we call the X-shaped cross the "St. Andrew's Cross." Because of the identification of relics of Andrew's body with Scotland during the Middle Ages, the St. Andrew's Cross is incorporated into much of the Scottish heraldry. Nearly all of the crack Scottish regiments proudly bear the St. Andrew's Cross in their crests, and the Union Jack, the British flag, is given its distinctive design by the blue-and-white St. Andrew's Cross under the St. George's and St. Patrick's Crosses.

Andrew hung on an X-shaped cross, but he was tied instead of nailed in order to prolong his agony. If the reports are true, he lingered for several days, faithful to Jesus Christ to the end. How does one "explain" such a man as Andrew?

In Copley Square, Boston, there is a statue of Phillips Brooks, the famous minister and author of "O Little Town of Bethlehem." Behind it there is another statue, the figure of Jesus Christ. The hand of Christ is resting on Brooks, driving him out into the passing crowd.

Years ago, a furor arose over the larger figure of Christ on the monument. Some sophisticated Bostonians wanted the Brooks statue to stand alone. He needed no Man of Nazareth behind him, they insisted. When their protests were ignored, they raised subscriptions and erected a new statue a few blocks away. This time, there was no Christ. Majestic, splendid, and alone, there was only Phillips Brooks.

Days passed, and so did the people—without noticing the new statue. It was finally removed because it was basically a falsehood. The only way to explain or understand Brooks was through Jesus Christ.

Andrew can only be explained by Jesus Christ. Apart from Him, Andrew's life is meaningless. Because of Jesus Christ, Andrew lived up to his name, "brave."

That same Jesus Christ is the only way you can be "explained." Apart from Him, you are useless. Without His hand on you, your life is empty. Alone, your life is a lie. With this same Jesus Christ, however, you have courage and purpose. Even though you may be overshadowed by others who get the honors and the headlines, with Jesus Christ you have life. What more can you want?

4

Nicodemus

NO ONE knows exactly why he sneaked out to see Jesus that night. Was it mere curiosity? Was it genuine interest? Was he a semiofficial deputy from the supreme court, the Sanhedrin, sent to interview Jesus? Was he intending to give advice to the young Rabbi from Galilee?

Like a character in a cloak-and-dagger production, Nicodemus slips in and out of the scenes in the Gospel of John. There is an air of mystery about him. Although he turns up only three times in the New Testament, there is obviously more to him than meets the eye; Nicodemus seems to be wrapped up in Jesus' career, even though his appearances seem casual and minor.

It was highly irregular for Nicodemus to visit Jesus. A member of "the Establishment" in Jerusalem, Nicodemus was a man with a genuine pedigree; he was wellborn and wealthy, one of the aristocracy. Nicodemus years earlier had joined that select company of six thousand dedicated Jews known as Pharisees. These Pharisees (the name meant "separated ones") sweated to observe every minor footnote of the Jewish law and enjoyed immense prestige for their pains. Later, Nicodemus was honored by being selected "a ruler of the Jews" (John 3:1), one of the Sanhedrin. The Sanhedrin was the most distinguished and most powerful body in the Jewish nation. As a supreme court, the Sanhedrin held life and death powers over every Jew in the world. Only seventy men held this honor. They were selected for their scholarship, leadership, and proven abilities. Nicodemus was well known around Jerusalem, and it was very unusual for a man of his standing and reputation to seek out a young Rabbi of dubious reputation from that hotbed of heresy, Galilee.

This was especially true after what the young Galilean Rabbi had done only a few days earlier. Jesus had enraged the Sanhedrin by marching right into the Temple precincts and driving out the money-changers and hucksters. Previously, Jesus had seemed simply a gadfly; after the Temple episode, He was a threat. The Sanhedrin, the Temple, the traditions—all the institutions that Nicodemus and the other sixty-nine rulers lived for—had been challenged. The brash young Rabbi was more than a nuisance; He was openly attacking the very foundations of their religion. A showdown was inevitable. Either He would have to go or they would have to change, and the Sanhedrin had no intention of changing. They marked Jesus for trial and bided their time. They had had enough of the Troublemaker from Galilee and were determined to silence Him once and for all.

Nicodemus came to see Jesus long after dark. Perhaps, as some think, Nicodemus came at night because he wanted to find Jesus at a time when He would not be distracted by others. Knowing how Jesus was in the middle of throngs of people all day, Nicodemus wanted a chance to talk without being disturbed and interrupted.

There seems to be more to it than simply a desire for privacy. Nicodemus shrouded his visit in secrecy. He did not want to be seen. He furtively came at night to escape detection. What an uproar would have followed if it became known that one of the august Sanhedrin had talked with Jesus! Nicodemus guarded his own reputation. Perhaps he reasoned that an interview with Jesus could be easily misconstrued. The wily old Sanhedrin wanted no misunderstandings.

We still have not answered the question, Why did he come in the first place? One school of thought maintains that Nicodemus was an emissary from the Sanhedrin who was sent to have an informal, off-the-record talk with Jesus. His opening words to Jesus were, ". . . we know that you are a teacher . . ." (John 3:2), and the use of "we" hints that he was speaking for others as well as himself. Was Nicodemus delegated to warn Jesus, or to counsel Him?

Or, as others think, did Nicodemus come on his own? If so, did he come as an old hand who knew the tricky ins and outs of Jerusalem politics? Maybe he felt that Jesus could use some pointers. Did he, the older, more experienced man of the world, come to offer his advice to One he felt was inexperienced and green? Did he have a proposed course of action for Jesus? Or was Nicodemus a man who wanted to see for himself what Jesus was like?

There is some indication that Nicodemus was honestly not sure what to make of Jesus. Perhaps he was uneasy with the "party line" that the Sanhedrin had adopted. A puzzled, honest seeker, Nicodemus was open-minded enough to risk his reputation and give up a night's sleep to talk with Jesus. He had heard the claims that Jesus was making. He had heard the claims his colleagues in the Sanhedrin were making. Nicodemus was not one to be swayed by public opinion. Some were ready to condemn Jesus, others were ready to worship Him as the Deliverer. Nicodemus felt he had a responsibility to find out for himself who Jesus was and what He was up to. As a leader of the land, one whose words carried great weight, he wanted to get the facts firsthand.

Other Pharisees had written off Jesus as One deserving the death penalty, but Nicodemus kept an open mind. An open mind is all that God asks of any doubter. When anyone is prejudiced against knowing Him, Jesus will mean little; He will only puzzle and threaten. God asks only that the skeptic be honest.

"Rabbi, we know that you are a teacher come from God; for no one can do these signs that you do, unless God is with him," Nicodemus said (John 3:2). These were flattering words coming from a leading judge, scholar, and religious leader. For a young peasant-bred Rabbi from the hinterland, they should have been as pleasant as honey. Nicodemus, the mellow old jurist and professor, was impressed by Jesus' miracles and was conferring a particularly graceful compliment. That nicety out of the way, Nicodemus prepared to settle down to a relaxed chat. He was certain that he, the famous, learned oldster, would be given a certain amount of deference by the young Teacher, especially since he had condescended to look up Jesus.

The old fellow was startled by Jesus' reply. Instead of recognizing His guest as one of the most distinguished men of the times, Jesus was not one bit impressed. In fact, He is not impressed by anyone's accomplishments. No matter how outstanding our credentials are, Jesus casually tosses them to one side and says, "They really don't mean a thing to Me. You need help. And through Me, God will give it to you."

Jesus brusquely ignored the bouquet of pretty words Nicodemus had handed Him and switched the subject. Nicodemus had remarked that important people were impressed by Jesus' wonders. This noncommittal, tea-table talk meant nothing to Jesus. His miracles were not crowd-gathering sensations performed by a religious stuntman. What Jesus really cared about was whether or not a man was right with God, and been changed by Him. ". . . unless one is born anew," He bluntly told Nicodemus, "he cannot see the kingdom of God" (v. 3).

Being impressed with Jesus is never enough. He did not

come to impress people, but to save them. He really did not care whether anyone was awed by His wonders. They were only "signs" indicating what God was doing through Jesus; the wonders in themselves were not important. Most important was the radical transformation God wanted to work in a man's life—this was the real miracle. The wonders Jesus worked pointed to the God who brings new life to men.

Jesus was determined to shake Nicodemus. Nicodemus had built himself a comfortable nest of tradition, dogma, regulation, institutionalism, and religious jargon. He had hung a "Do Not Disturb" sign on his religion. "I'm snoozing contentedly and don't want to be upset," Nicodemus was thinking. "I am confident that I have done all I need to do, and have learned everything I need to learn. After all, I am a member of the Sanhedrin."

Many of us think like Nicodemus. We convince ourselves that traditions, accomplishments, honors, and learning are what count in the world. Belonging to the right club, keeping the right rules, accepting the proper doctrines, repeating the proper teachings—these convince us that God is with us. Jesus tore apart Nicodemus' smug religion. He warns us that it is not enough to be simply "a good Presbyterian" or anything else.

"Unless one is born anew . . . ," Jesus says. How radical! Isn't it enough to be patched up? "Born anew" sounds so drastic. But Jesus means to be drastic with us. We need an entirely new outlook, a wholly new personality, a completely new nature. Merely tinkering around with ourselves is not enough.

Nicodemus was bewildered. "Born anew" had a double meaning. The words, of course, could mean literally going through the process of physical birth once more. In Greek, they could mean that. In Greek, however, they could also mean, "born *from above*." Nicodemus took the words in a narrow, literal sense and was completely mystified. Perhaps he thought for an instant that Jesus meant something about reincarnation, but he remembered the words, "born anew." Puzzled and disconcerted, Nicodemus asked how anyone, especially an old man like himself, could ever hope to start over again in life, beginning with the process of birth.

There is a wistful note to Nicodemus' words. He betrays that he would like to start all over again in life. If only he could have a second chance, how much he would do differently. With startling realism, Nicodemus speaks longingly of beginning once more as a newborn infant. "If only I could turn the clock back. . . ." "If only I hadn't done that. . . ." "If only . . ."—we realize too late how many precious opportunities we waste. We race through the years without really living.

One of the most moving scenes in Thornton Wilder's *Our Town* is when Emily is allowed to return from the cemetery to relive a day from her earlier existence in Grovers Corners. She finally selects her twelfth birthday, and steps back into time fourteen years earlier. It is a typical day in a typical household: her mother busies herself with housework and her father is preoccupied with business. No one pays much attention to anyone else and each takes the others somewhat for granted. Emily finally sobs, "Oh, it goes so fast. We don't have time to look at one another. . . . Do human beings ever realize life while they live in it?—every, every minute?"

Occasionally we all have moments like Emily's. There is nothing that we would like more than to start over. Plaintively, Nicodemus wondered aloud the same thing.

A new life an impossibility? Nothing, Jesus made it clear, is impossible with God. He breaks through and does what we least expect. In fact, Jesus told Nicodemus, ". . . unless one is born of water and the Spirit, he cannot enter the kingdom of God" (John 3:5).

Water symbolized cleansing. "Born of water" meant that God wipes out the guilt and fears of our pasts. God forgives, and a new page is spread before us.

"Born of the Spirit" means that God's presence and power take hold of us and do what we can never do for ourselves. Until we personally experience His forgiveness and until we personally are renewed by His Spirit, we are not able to live under God in trust and obedience.

You and I were created once, and we arrived once in this world. Perhaps it was twenty, thirty, sixty-five years ago; it makes no difference. The point is that God means for you and me to know a new birthday. Recreated by the Spirit, we are meant to arrive in this world as different persons, as people whom the Spirit has refashioned.

This is God's doing, not yours or mine. Just as you and I had nothing to do with our passing from our mothers' wombs into this world, so we can not remake ourselves into better people. God is the Doer, not man. We erroneously think that Christianity is a self-improvement course where we can make ourselves more interesting, more attractive, more intelligent. Jesus is not asking us to sign up at a charm school; He is not instructing us to polish ourselves up.

We must understand that we are sinners. If we think we can make ourselves into wise, charming, thoughtful persons, we are really saying that we do not need God. We are assuming that we can save ourselves by our own goodness and our own wisdom. Jesus repeats, "You must be born anew." Only God can re-create. Only as He renews us will we be saved.

Born anew! It's the same world, but we see it afresh. We are born into it as different persons, once the Spirit takes hold of us.

Saul Kane, in John Masefield's "The Everlasting Mercy," was a roistering, drunken, hard-punching drifter. Then, dramatically transformed by Jesus Christ, he cried,

> I knew that Christ had given me birth
> To brother all the souls on earth,

Because of His everlasting mercy which had given Kane a new birth, even familiar sights were changed:

> The station brook, to my new eyes,
> Was babbling out of Paradise,
> The waters rushing from the rain
> Were singing Christ has risen again.

An oldster, Nicodemus thinks at a plodding pace. He cannot keep up with the agility of Jesus' mind. Like so many people past thirty, Nicodemus finds himself nearly incapable of receiving a new idea. "What a good thing it would be if every scientific man was to die when sixty years old, as afterward he would be sure to oppose all new doctrines," wrote Charles Darwin in bitterness and in truth. It is hard to look at facts with a new point of view. Nicodemus' thinking processes creak as he tries to take hold of what Jesus has told him: "Born anew . . . born of water and the Spirit . . . the Spirit."

The Spirit? Nicodemus, a student of the Book, an expert on the law, is perplexed. He spills out his misgivings and doubts. How does the Spirit operate? How do I know Him?

Perhaps they sat on a housetop. Possibly they were near some olive trees. The night breeze brushed their faces and stirred the leaves. Explain the Spirit's working? You're just as likely to be able to give a satisfying explanation of that wind, or where it comes from, how it blows, where it goes after touching your face, was Jesus' answer. The Hebrew and Greek words for "Spirit" and "wind" are one and the same. Both wind and Spirit are "there"; you know that, yet you cannot see where either comes from or how either works. We do not understand everything about His operations, but the Spirit's power and nearness in our lives are as obvious as the wind rustling the leaves in the trees.

There comes a point where we must stop theorizing about the Almighty's traits and allow ourselves to receive the Spirit's mercy and power. Jesus made it clear that it was time for Nicodemus to do exactly that. Reading books, discussing profound issues, arguing ethics, and watching Jesus' wonders are not enough. We are meant to have more than secondhand, book-report, hearsay knowledge of God.

Then Jesus disclosed to Nicodemus that through Him, Jesus of Nazareth, there is firsthand knowledge of God. Gray-bearded Nicodemus had come that night to meet One he supposed to be a callow, inexperienced Rabbi. Nicodemus had assumed that he, the learned and venerable Sanhedrinist, would be doing the teaching. Instead, he was the instructed, and he heard the most daring, the most vital announcement of his life. Jesus revealed that He was "he who descended from heaven, the Son of man" (John 3:13).

Next Jesus spoke of why He had come: His mission was one of mercy to a dying, hopeless world. He referred to the plight the Israelites had once suffered during their wanderings in the desert under Moses. Desperately ill from the bites of poisonous desert vipers, they were visited by God and commanded to look on a brass serpent lifted up on a pole. Jesus announced to the astonished Nicodemus that His mission was exactly the same. He would be lifted up and anyone looking to Him would be saved.

"It was as a physician and not as a judge that He had come," as St. Chrysostom so beautifully described the meaning of Jesus' coming into our world. John, the disciple-writer who was present during the conversation between Nicodemus and Jesus, sums it up best: "For God so loved the world, that he gave his only begotten Son, that whosoever believeth in him should not perish, but have everlasting life" (John 3:16, KJV).

Nicodemus left that evening only partially understanding Jesus. Although he was impressed, he had not been able to bring himself to an all-out act of commitment to Jesus as Deliverer. He tried to show his respect for Jesus and at the same time remain a member in good standing of the Sanhedrin. It proved to be impossible.

The chasm between Jesus and the national leaders widened and deepened. The members of the Sanhedrin were furious at Jesus' challenge to their power and prestige; most were ready to vote the death penalty even before they convened officially as a court of the Sanhedrin. They sent officers to bring charges and put Jesus under arrest. When the arresting officers returned empty-handed and full of praises for Jesus, the Sanhedrinists were in no mood to waste any more time on legal fine points. "Why did you not bring him?" they shrieked (John 7:45).

Nicodemus was a man with an uneasy conscience. He must have wanted to keep silent. He had met Jesus, however, and his partial loyalty made him speak up. Even so, he carefully chose his words. He put on a pose of righteousness and spoke as a member of the Sanhedrin. "Does our law," he pompously asked, "judge a man without first giving him a hearing and learning what he does?" (v. 51).

Nicodemus was trying to have it both ways: playing the part of a conscientious Pharisee and at the same time doing what he could for Jesus. His words have a courtroom ring. Nicodemus carefully avoided showing his leaning toward Jesus. He was not so much defending Jesus as he was trying to appear to defend justice.

Nicodemus preened himself inwardly on his clever stroke. Even if he were criticized, he could readily defend himself. After all, his job was to uphold justice; he was only doing his duty. He had made provision to protect his reputation and protect Jesus at the same time.

A compromise with Jesus always fails. Nicodemus' colleagues suspected his motives and threw the garbage of abuse and sarcasm. "Are you from Galilee too?" they taunted (v. 52). "Search and you will see that no prophet is to rise from Galilee." They not only accused him of being a fellow-traveler with Jesus but insulted his intelligence.

How did Nicodemus behave during the trial of Jesus? Did he keep quiet and thus condone the sentence? Did he protest the illegality of the trial? Where was his passion for justice that he had made so much of previously? Did he hesitate to take an unpopular stand? Did he remember his attempt to help Jesus—the ridicule, the suspicion? Had he been so stung on that painful occasion that he decided the best policy was to say nothing? We hear nothing of Nicodemus during Jesus' trial before the Sanhedrin.

We might expect Nicodemus to fade from the scene at this point. Strangely, however, he appears once more: Nicodemus came to Jesus' tomb after the crucifixion. Panting with exertion, the old man carried one hundred pounds of spices with which to anoint Jesus' body. It was an expensive tribute. Only a wealthy man could have afforded one hundred pounds of spices. For Nicodemus, it was a guilt-offering.

Nicodemus realized too late what had happened. He had had an opportunity to serve, but he had let it slip past. Then, it was too late. Guilt-ridden, Nicodemus thought back over the previous day. If he had spoken up, if he had organized a few of his fellow Sanhedrinists of similar sympathies to vote against sentencing Jesus! If, if, if! Carrying a hundred pounds of spices to place around a corpse was poor consolation for the failures of his past.

A heavy-hearted man, Nicodemus learned that carrying out funeral chores when a friend is dead is no substitute for showing concern for him when he is alive. All the tributes and eulogies in the world mean nothing compared to one word of love spoken when the friend is still living.

Thomas Carlyle knew Nicodemus' anguish. While his wife Jane was alive, Carlyle was curt and brusque with her. He was given to long, moody silences, and rebuffed her kindnesses. After her death, he found her diary and was stricken with despair as he discovered entries such as: "Oh, why can't you say something nice if I have pleased you in any way? Why must you be so moody and quiet? I am starving for one word of praise from you, yet you ignore everything I do to make you happier." Nicodemus was torn into pieces in the same way Carlyle was—and the way you or I are whenever we let our chances to serve another person slip by.

All the same, Nicodemus was a changed man. Instead of caution and timidity, Nicodemus was aflame with courage and resolve. At a time when not even Jesus' disciples could bring themselves to venture out from behind barred doors, Nicodemus—who had more to lose than these penniless nobodies—stood up for Jesus. Peter, James, John, Andrew, and the others were too cowed even to bury their Master. It was Nicodemus and another Sanhedrinist, Joseph of Arimathea, who undertook the risky chore. Nicodemus laid his position, his honors, his reputation, and his future on the block for the sake of one act of devotion to Jesus.

Nicodemus dirtied his hands literally and figuratively for Jesus. A burial detail is unpleasant work. For two older men not used to heavy physical exertion, carrying Jesus' dead body was exhausting. Worse, it polluted them. According to the strict ceremonial law which they knew by heart,

Nicodemus and Joseph of Arimathea were rendering themselves unclean. There were specific rules about handling the dead. Those who did were kept away from all religious ceremonies for days until the elaborate purification rites were carried out. Nicodemus was doing something no Jew would do at any time. This was particularly true at Passover time: coming in contact with a body meant that Nicodemus could not participate in the Passover celebration. Nicodemus was well aware of what he was doing, and he was willing to rule himself out of the most joyous and meaningful church festival and family holiday of the year.

Only one thing can explain the change that came over Nicodemus—the cross. The cross made Nicodemus a new man. To a strait-laced Jew, a cross would have meant nothing but disgrace and scandal. Amazingly, however, Jesus' cross came to mean divine suffering and love. It cracked Nicodemus' pride and legalism once and for all.

Nicodemus was one of the first men to be brought into new life because of the cross. He remembered the night when he had first met Jesus. Did he recall Jesus' reference to Moses holding the brass serpent on a pole, and the pointed remark that He too would be lifted up so that all who looked on Him would find health and life? Nicodemus had known Jesus lifted up on a pole called a cross. Love so amazing, so divine, demanded Nicodemus' life, his soul, his all.

Jesus died on that pole, but Nicodemus was born anew.

5

Zacchaeus

AN HONEST tax collector was such a rare specimen that one Roman reported seeing a statue erected to a tax collector who did not cheat! Murderers, thieves, and tax collectors were always classified together by the rabbis.

Taxes in Jesus' day were staggeringly heavy. To begin with, there was a head tax on every man from the age of fourteen to sixty-five, and on every woman from twelve to sixty-five. Then there was a tax of one per cent of a man's income. Nearly everybody farmed, and that meant paying the ground tax of one-tenth of all grain grown and one-fifth of all oil and wine pressed. There was a tax on each wheel of a cart, another tax on each animal pulling the cart. Tolls were levied on people using most of the roads and markets. Many items in the markets had a purchase tax attached. People had to pay duty on many articles that were imported, and there was even duty charged on articles that were exported.

The Roman system of tax collection was notoriously conducive to dishonesty. The Romans simply farmed out the actual work of collecting the assessments. A tax collector bought the appointment at a fat price, then went about regaining his investment as fast as he could. There were few safeguards against overcharging and corruption; all Rome cared about was receiving the correct amount of money. How the taxes were collected and how much went into the pockets of the collectors were of no concern to the government. The system had built-in possibilities for every kind of abuse. Unless a tax collector literally ruined the economy of a country, he knew his chances were good to go on over-charging for years without being exposed. There was little the average citizen could do except pay; behind the tax collector stood the might of the Roman legions.

Tax collectors were given a great deal of latitude. They could even stop a man on the road, make him unpack his load, and charge him just about anything they pleased. Frequently, tax collectors were moneylenders. They would make loans to those unable to pay their taxes, then charge exorbitant interest rates.

Tax collectors were directly or indirectly implicated with almost every sordid crime in the book. Extortion, kick-backs, graft, shakedowns, and usury were their stocks-in-trade. Because they sold their services to the hated Romans, they were quislings in the eyes of everybody else.

Jericho was a juicy plum for a tax collector. A rich oasis with an ideal climate, it was surrounded by groves of date palms and balsams. Jericho exported dates and "balm of Gilead" to all points in the Middle East. One of the wealthiest cities of the day, it was described as the "fattest in Palestine" by the contemporary historian Josephus. Jericho was located on the main north-south trade route between Egypt and Judea, and therefore it was a key customs station. The customs office was so busy that it took a team of tax collectors to handle the revenue. The chief of this operation was exceptionally well fixed—and well hated. Zacchaeus was his name. His name means "pure" in Hebrew, but it had become a bitter joke in Jericho.

Although he had been born a Jew, Zacchaeus had forfeited his standing in the community and his faith when he became a tax collector—tax collectors were automatically drummed out of membership in the synagogue. Ostracized as a turncoat, shunned as a loan shark, excluded as a cheat, resented as a rich money-grabber, Zacchaeus would have been better off as a leper. He could buy anything he wanted except what he needed and wanted most—a friend.

He had all the leisure, wealth, comforts, and security any man could desire; yet he was dissatisfied. When he heard that the young Rabbi from Galilee was going to pass through Jericho, Zacchaeus was interested. Perhaps he thought it would be an afternoon's diversion to see this Jesus everybody was talking about. He had not the foggiest hope that Jesus could ever do anything for him.

Zacchaeus was as welcome to his fellow townsmen as a fire in the balsam groves. When he tried to get a place along the road to see Jesus, he was not only shunned; he was literally elbowed out. No one moved aside to let him see, or offered him a place. A short man, Zacchaeus knew that he would never be able to see over that crowd.

Zacchaeus was a positive, direct person. He was used to making quick decisions. Couldn't see Jesus because of the crowds? He solved that problem with typical decisiveness: he climbed a tree along the road.

Then began a series of events that made that day the most significant in Zacchaeus' life. The first amazing thing was that Jesus stopped under Zacchaeus' tree and called him by name. (When Jesus summons a man, He speaks to him directly and personally.) The second amazing thing was that Jesus invited himself to dinner at Zacchaeus' house.

How did Jesus know Zacchaeus' name? Had He overheard people sneering, "There goes that dirty racketeer Zacchaeus! Serves him right, having to climb that tree!"? Was Zacchaeus so well known as chief tax collector of Jericho that Jesus had heard of his reputation and name? Had Jesus run into Zacchaeus before? Perhaps the former tax collector called Levi, who became the disciple Matthew, told Jesus to look up his old crony Zacchaeus when He went through Jericho. Perhaps Jesus had already inquired where

He could find Zacchaeus, and someone pointed to the tree and said, "There he is. See? Up in that tree. That's Zacchaeus!"

Jesus called to the hated, greedy tax collector, "Zacchaeus, make haste and come down; for I must stay at your house today" (Luke 19:5). This was the turning point in Zacchaeus' life.

Jesus found Zacchaeus on a perch, detached from the world, proud that he was "above" the crowd; Zacchaeus in that tree was separated from the world. Once Jesus called him, he was no longer able to view the scene as a haughty, superior observer, looking down on everyone else. "Come down!" Jesus commanded.

Once we are found by Jesus, we are no longer permitted our pleasant, shaded, grandstand seats in life. Jesus calls us down to the hot street with the rest of mankind, to the dusty road of life where He Himself is.

"Today," Jesus announced to Zacchaeus, "I must stay at your house." Zacchaeus clambered down from the tree and joyously invited Jesus to come to his home.

Jesus wants to go home with us. Unless He is allowed in our homes, He will never be real to us.

One of the things that continually amazes us about Jesus is His ability to get close to people, particularly those we might label "problem cases"—the emotionally disturbed, prostitutes, racketeers, the criminal fringe. Anyone who does counseling can verify that it is especially difficult to get close to these people. Jesus had the unique faculty of not only gaining their confidence but bringing them into a new relationship with God and the world.

One clue is Jesus' genuine interest in people. He is the Friend. Often, you and I think we must "help" someone, but we cannot seem to "get to" those who need help. Part of the reason is that we go as scolds, or superiors, or judges; we only increase the other person's resentment and resistance. People are rightfully suspicious of do-gooders and character-improvers. Not even His enemies ever called Jesus such names.

The crowd called Jesus plenty of other names, however, when He went off to Zacchaeus' house. As John Wycliffe, who first translated the Bible into English, put it, everybody in Jericho was "grucchynge" (grouching) at Jesus. "He has gone in to be the guest of a man who is a sinner" (Luke 19:7).

Most famous men stay around on Main Street, playing to the hilt the role of popular idol. Lunch with the mayor is the proper procedure, then a public reception for the civic leaders, and some more mingling with the crowds. Following that, there might be a huge testimonial banquet.

Jesus was so well known that the town had turned out to line the street, but He took note of Jericho's most unpopular, disreputable inhabitant and deliberately chose to spend His time with him. What kind of a "religious" man was this Jesus? Jericho asked itself. Consorting with Zacchaeus! Even eating with a shyster like that! The leading citizens were indignant and hurt and annoyed. What kind of an example was Jesus setting for good citizenship? How could they ever get some justice in Jericho, how could they ever get an adjustment in the unfair tax rates while Jesus hung around with Zacchaeus?

Jesus defined popular opinion and risked getting a bad reputation. "A man is known by the company he keeps"; "Birds of a feather flock together"—there are counterparts of these homely sayings in every language. Jesus was well aware of what Jericho was saying. "They all say" is one of the strongest forces in the world, and one that leaves few of us unmoved.

Jesus risked His reputation, His dignity—everything—for the sake of one greedy racketeer. Sitting down at a table with a tax collector meant losing all respectability and pride. Breaking bread with someone, in Jewish life, was a sacred thing; a "good" Jew never ate with someone who broke the commandments. Jesus was willing to associate with Zacchaeus and make Himself a "bad" Jew. Jesus became an outcast for the sake of an outcast. In fact, Jesus became the ultimate in outcasts; he was finally cast out on a cross for the sake of all the world's Zacchaeuses.

"He has gone in to be the guest of a man who is a sinner," they grouched. What self-righteousness! Zacchaeus was a sinner—*they*, of course, were not! At least that is what they assumed. In reality, we *all* are sinners. No person should dare call another a sinner without first remembering that the badge is also pinned on his own lapel.

We forget that God chose as His own those sinners who were willing to admit they were sinners. Many of them hardly approached our ideas of goodness at all: Abraham was a liar; Jacob was a thief; Moses was a murderer; Rahab was a harlot; David was an adulterer.

Zacchaeus' hometown was remembered as the city that Joshua attacked so brilliantly years earlier. The walls around Jericho came tumbling down under Joshua's relentless siege. Zacchaeus, however, would remember Jericho as the place where the walls around his personality came tumbling down under Jesus' interest and friendship.

There had been many walls around Zacchaeus' personality. He was short; he felt inferior; he had built a wall of resentment toward others. He had been booted out of the synagogue, and this erected a wall of self-pity. Zacchaeus was rich, and wealth makes walls even where there is no dishonesty. He was avoided by others, rudely shoved aside when he tried to mingle with his townspeople. A wall of loneliness rose up. Beyond all those walls, the world lost sight of the man Zacchaeus. From behind all those walls, Zacchaeus in turn could not see others. He lived in lonely, miserable seclusion, even though he was surrounded by people all day. Jesus broke down those walls by coming and inviting Himself into Zacchaeus' life.

You and I can find the same thing to be true today! When we realize that Jesus Christ still stands, speaking our names, inviting Himself into our lives, the walls around us come tumbling down.

Once a person knows the mercy of God in Jesus Christ, there will be a response in him. Zacchaeus felt the concern of Christ. "Then," he thought, "I'll be His. To show my gratitude, here's my bank account." There was no hedging, no equivocating, no playing it safe. What a contrast to our rabbitlike timidity! Zacchaeus made an enthusiastic commitment to a go-for-broke discipleship. In spite of the humiliation of making restitution and facing the people day in and day out, Zacchaeus was honest at last with everyone.

There are three types of giving: (1) "I have to," or compulsion; (2) "I ought to," or obligation; (3) "I want to," or response. Christian giving is the third; the first two are somewhat pagan. Zacchaeus' giving was the "I want to" type. We could paraphrase John's words, "We love, because he first loved us" (I John 4:19), to "we give, because He first gave to us."

Zachaeus responded by turning over to Jesus and others what formerly had meant most to him—his money. Jesus is the Saviour, and He saved Zacchaeus from hoarding. Zacchaeus then became a trustee of his possessions. He knew he was no longer an owner, but simply a steward. For Zacchaeus, money became not something to be accumulated and guarded, but something to be shared. He learned the privilege of giving. "Behold, Lord, the half of my goods I give to the poor; and if I have defrauded any one of anything, I restore it fourfold" (Luke 19:8), Zacchaeus promised.

The more we know of God's mercy, the more we respond

by sharing—even our money. Money is what we are most loath to share; it is easier to rationalize when it comes to our checkbooks. We are willing to discuss practically any phase of our response to Jesus Christ, except the financial. Money is the touchy area, and here we grow defensive.

We spend nine times as much on alcoholic beverages each year in the United States as on Christian church giving; about seven times as much on tobacco products as on church giving. We Americans spend five times more for water sports than for our church, four times more on beauty aids, two times more on movie tickets. We paid about an equal amount on bowling as we gave last year to all our Christian churches. Our national gambling bill, even by conservative estimates, is about fifteen times as much as our total church giving.

"Money talks," states the old saw. Money *does* talk—about us! According to the *Southern Baptist Handbook*, Mr. Average American spends only five cents a day for religious and welfare causes. In contrast to this nickel, he spends nine cents daily for tobacco, fifteen cents for alcoholic beverages, twenty-two cents for recreation. At the same time, we like to think of ourselves as "a Christian nation," and pride ourselves that nearly all (over 96 per cent) of us Mr. Average Americans claim to be firm believers in God.

More money is spent on astrology in the United States than is spent on world evangelism each year. This is a sign that too many of us think God is dead or silent. In our land of conspicuous consumption, we think nothing of spending three quarters of a billion dollars just to play golf each year. Take a couple of other examples: in 1960, we spent $200 million to buy ribbon and paper to wrap our Christmas presents, $42 million for cat food, $35 million for hair tinting. That same year, the United Presbyterian Church squeezed and strained to give a little over $30 million to its general mission budget. The record for the Methodists, Baptists, Lutherans, Episcopalians, Church of Christ, and other Protestant bodies is about the same.

When Christian missionaries were first pushing through the German forests to bring the gospel to the wild Teutonic tribes, certain chiefs often agreed to Christian baptism for themselves and their followers, but with one proviso! they insisted on keeping their sword arms high above the water when immersed. In this way, they maintained, they could go on with the bloody warfare they had waged as pagans because their sword arms had never been baptized.

We Christians today need to have our purses baptized. Our giving shows unmistakably that we have not understood that a response to the gospel means giving our money as well as the rest of us. We are stingy; we are reluctant to share; we are resentful of having to respond to God's grace with our money. Money is the dirty word in American church-life today.

There is a direct tie-in between how much we are aware of God's grace and how much of our incomes we share. God gave; if we know this, we too must give. And this giving must include what means so much to us: money.

Zacchaeus did not drift off into pipe dreams about how he'd like to build a hospital or endow a university. "It's not what you'd do if a million were your lot; it's what you do with the quarter-dollar that you've got."

Each year, the Board of National Missions of the United Presbyterian Church receives a unique gift. It is a package of one or two white fox skins sent by Charles Slwooko, of Gambell, St. Lawrence Island, Alaska. Mr. Slwooko is a hunter and trapper in the barren, treacherous Bering Straits. His first gift of furs to the Board of National Missions arrived in New York over fifteen years ago, wrapped in a sugar sack and accompanied with a note that read something like this:

"I had much owe at store. I have big family to feed and no money. I not know where to turn. Very few fox caught. I pray the Lord to help me to get food for family. I went out and set my traps. In three weeks I caught ninety foxes. I pay my owe at the store. I buy food for my family. Praise the Lord. He can do anything. In thanks I send fox fur to Board of National Missions."

"Nature knows nothing of rich men. She bore all of us poor," observed St. Ambrose in the fourth century. We might go a step further: we only remember rich men who have given away their money. Drew, Vanderbilt, and Stanford are remembered today chiefly as names of universities. Although each of these institutions was started through the bequest of a multimillionaire, who remembers much—if anything—about these men? Guggenheim and Russell Sage are forgotten today except as the names of foundations. Huntington is renowned primarily as the name of a Library. Perhaps the same will be true of Rockefeller and Ford in another hundred years.

Zacchaeus was specific, direct, and immediate. His giving was systematic and proportionate. We don't know what people said about Zacchaeus one hundred years later, but we do know what Jesus said about him that evening. "Today," Jesus announced, "salvation has come to this house, since he also is a son of Abraham. For the Son of man came to seek and to save the lost" (Luke 19:9-10).

Jesus gave Zacchaeus a new status. Others had banned Zacchaeus, a son of Abraham, from the community of Israel. Jesus announced that Zacchaeus was not only restored to that community but was no less a son of Abraham than the others.

Jesus seeks out lost people like Zacchaeus. "Lost" here

means "misplaced," not "condemned" or "doomed." Zacchaeus was lost in the same way a sheep was lost from the shepherd's flock, or a coin was lost from the dowry headpiece of a peasant woman in Jesus' parables (Luke 15).

Jesus did not come primarily as Teacher, to philosophize. He did not come as Advisor, to give more rules. He did not come as Encourager, to dispense pep talks and cheery words. "For the Son of man is come to seek and to save that which was lost" (KJV).

Zacchaeus did not choose Jesus; rather, Jesus chose Zacchaeus. We talk of "seeking God," but it is always God who is seeking us. It is we who are lost, not God.

Some have grown sentimental over Zacchaeus. Some have gushed, "Zacchaeus was really a nice man at heart, and had been all the time." Feeling sorry for Zacchaeus, some say he was a poor fellow who was never understood or appreciated by the people of Jericho. One school of thought maintains that Jesus always finds a vein of goodness and kindness in everybody, and that He uncovered this in Zacchaeus.

We must not romanticize either Zacchaeus' story or our own stories. There has been too much sentimental slop written about the nobility and dignity and charity of man. Human nature is not fundamentally good, and it is high time we stopped beating around the bush. We are in need of the Saviour. All the talk about our being so noble and dignified and good is empty prattle. Let us clearly understand that Jesus does not come to refine some already existent ore of kindness in us. Anyone who thinks this has missed the point of the cross and the resurrection: Jesus Christ came as our *Saviour*.

Those in the man-is-so-good school of thought do not believe they need Him as Saviour. Man, they say, is able to save himself by his own charm, his own wisdom, his own attractiveness. God's message throughout the Scriptures is that man is not—repeat, *not*—able to save himself. Neither by his brains, brawn, beauty, goodness, piety, or anything else in man, can he be saved.

Zacchaeus did not charm Jesus with his winsome personality. Zacchaeus was not such a fine man underneath it all that Jesus was "wowed." Rather, Jesus sought and saved a tax collector who was a sinner.

One of the last ships to pull into the blazing ruins of Dunkirk during the gallant evacuation of the British Army in 1940 was the destroyer *H.M.S. Malcolm.* At tremendous risk, the *Malcolm* picked its way among the forest of sunken ships and moored at the end of a blasted quay. It was early dawn. Not a man could be seen waiting to be taken off the beach.

The surviving soldiers in Dunkirk had collapsed into comalike sleep from exhaustion and hunger. Dispirited and forsaken, they had given up hope of being evacuated. They were certain that they had been left behind, and expected only death or a prison camp.

The men on the *Malcolm* wondered where the remaining troops were. Then the navigator of the *Malcolm*, a young Scotsman named Ian Cox, did an amazing thing. Leaping from the ship to the quay with his bagpipes, Cox calmly started playing his pipes and boldly marched into the ruined city. In spite of bursting shells, he advanced up one street and down another, seeking out hopeless, sleeping men with a lilting, insistent, familiar tune. Men who thought they had been forgotten and abandoned, men who had crawled away to hide and die, men who had given up were brought to their feet and given new energy. Still piping, Cox led them back to the *Malcolm* and to the safety of home.

God came to seek and save dispirited, hopeless men. At immense personal sacrifice, He got down here among us in the dust, destruction, and death of our world. In the Person of Jesus, God marched up to us in our loneliness and misery. With a lilting, insistent plea, Jesus called men to be with

Him. Men who had given up—or men the world had given up on—were brought out of the stupor of selfishness and despair.

He seeks us. With Him, we are brought to new life. By Him, we are saved!

6

The Rich Young Ruler

HE IS not yet forty, but he has fulfilled all his college dreams. He is married to an attractive, well-dressed woman, and they have two lovely children. Their house is suburban split-level; the decor, Early American. A red sports car for him to tool around in on Sunday mornings, and a station wagon for the wife to use to chauffeur and shop, occupy the driveway beside the spacious, well-tended yard. A membership at the country club means that he swims, golfs, and attends dances on most week-ends. He wears the proper uniform: ivy-league cut with subdued striped tie and an air of confidence, authority, and prosperity. Already a member of the Junior Chamber of Commerce, he is talked about as a Successful Young Man on His Way Up. In the words he and his roommates used back at school, he "has it made." Yet he vaguely senses that something is lacking.

As he moves casually toward the group in conversation there is an unmistakable atmosphere of success about our man. It is as unostentatious as his tailoring, but as obvious as his good grooming. His words quickly show that he has a keen mind, enjoys exchanging opinions, has had a course which the catalogue of his university listed as "Comparative Religion I."

"Good Teacher," he coolly inquires, "what must I do to inherit eternal life?" (Mark 10:17). He is the rich young ruler who in every generation decides to take a look at Jesus.

"*Good* Teacher . . . ," he says, injecting a subtle note of flattery. Jesus stops him cold; compliments are like confetti and Jesus brushes them away. The young man, faintly patronizing, uses the term "Good Teacher" as an empty gesture. Jesus does not want anyone's patronage; nor does He want to be given the title of "good" unless the speaker means it.

Our young man wants some good advice, maybe a "thought for the day," perhaps even a weighty pronouncement. Obviously, he does not want an insistent demand from God for his obedience.

It might be interesting to have a friendly chat with Jesus, a stimulating interchange of ideas. The up-and-coming young man enjoys a good discussion on religion, and "eternal life" is a meaty subject for theorizing. Our man, however, wants to talk about it in the abstract. His relationship to God is something to be discussed, not lived.

". . . what good thing shall I do, that I may have eternal life?" (Matthew 19:16, KJV), or literally, in the Greek, "What one good thing must I do . . . ?" Donate a room at the hospital? Write a sizable check for the Community Chest? What one good thing must I do to solve the problem of eternal life?

The well-to-do young man assumes that he can "get" eternal life by what *he* does. Notice that he says nothing about what God does; it is what he thinks he can do. (Significantly, the rich young ruler never mentions God directly or indirectly during the entire interview!) He is cocksure that he can impress God by what he does. God, in this man's thinking, will surely reward him for being so irresistibly good. This is the "merit badge" idea of salvation: earn enough credits by what you do and God will be delighted to pin an award of eternal life on you and proudly shake your hand.

This is the height of conceit, this Look-God-am-I-not-a-good-guy idea of salvation. This is a man who really does not need a Saviour. He is confident that he can handle his life quite adequately himself.

Jesus does not play the man's little game. At the same time, Jesus does not turn His back on him. Taking in the kind of person He is dealing with, Jesus meets him on the plane where he has been thinking and tries to lead him into thinking about God instead of himself. "If you would enter life," Jesus answers, "keep the commandments" (Matthew 10:17).

What kind of Teacher is this Jesus, anyhow? ". . . keep the commandments"—that's the kind of answer they give kindergartners. First, Jesus was somewhat rude in calling him down for his genial greeting, "Good Teacher." Now He is refusing to go along with the young ruler's idea of a good discussion on religion. Keep the commandments indeed! What kind of deadbeat does Jesus think he is? And yet—the commandments—there are some which he would just as soon not discuss. It's unpleasant to have to drag up the past. He feels a twinge of guilt.

The young man thinks he can play around with academic questions as a dodge. ". . . keep the commandments," Jesus told him; that is, obey the will of God. The rich young ruler knows this, but he evades. Trapped by Jesus' answer, he squirms away, asking superciliously "which" commandment! (Matthew 19:18). He knows the commandments backwards and forwards already, but his question should get the heat off him. He feels somewhat satisfied that he has redeemed himself. His neat reply, "Which?" is rather clever: it poses new problems and raises additional intellectual questions; it puts Jesus on the defensive for a change, and gets the conversation back into safe waters.

Jesus sees that the man is artfully trying to dodge the real issue. This young ruler is too concerned about himself and his supposed spiritual and intellectual problems. He is trying to sidestep God's command by emphasizing human speculation. Avoiding the reality of God, he has been hiding under his doubts. It is much easier to talk about God and raise questions about Him than to trust Him and obey Him. Jesus knows this, and refuses to be distracted by the interesting side-issues that the young ruler brings up. Taking the offensive once more, Jesus exposes him completely. He simply quoted the commandments of God.

Our man is trapped again. Instead of treating his questions as the real issue, Jesus keeps treating him as the real issue. Jesus seems far more interested in a person than in a person's problems. He persists in turning the conversation around to how the young man must live before God. Jesus has put him on the spot again, clearly giving him no choice but to obey.

The rich young ruler makes a last desperate effort to bluff Jesus. Pretending to be unsatisfied with Jesus' answer, he acts as if he must pursue the matter further. Surely, this can't be all that God wants! He confidently expands as he relates that he has kept all the commandments from his youth. Now he is on safe ground; there is a note of satisfaction in his voice. No sir, he has never once killed, committed adultery, stolen, lied, cheated, or acted dishonorably toward his parents. That being so, he stands a bit straighter and states that surely there must be something more he can do, some unusual demand he can carry out. "What one thing special can I do?"

He is a man so determined to maintain his independence from God that he claims the revealed commandments of God are incomplete! Here also is a man who has confused respectability for trust, who has mistaken religion for obedience. The rich young ruler is a pillar in the community. He stands for all that is decent and proper. He is proud that he is so respectable. Furthermore, he is a "religious" man. He is satisfied that he always does exactly as he should.

Jesus is not in the least impressed. The man's Dun & Bradstreet rating and country club membership mean nothing to Him. The young ruler's pretense of piety fails to impress Jesus. His parade of respectability and religiosity simply exposes the self-deceit of our rich young friend. In short, he is a phony, a pretender.

Jesus knows him for exactly the fake he is. We might expect the next line in the gospel account to read, "And Jesus chewed him out," or "And Jesus turned away in disgust." Instead, there occurs one of the most meaningful sentences in the Bible: "And Jesus looking upon him loved him . . ." (Mark 10:21).

What relief these words are to us hypocrites! In spite of our self-deceit, in spite of our evasions and game-playing with Jesus Christ, He looks upon us and loves us! We need to remember this fact throughout the remainder of the interview, particularly when Jesus speaks His next words.

Jesus calls the young man's bluff. An extraordinary demand, is that what he wants? All right, Jesus says, I will give you the one thing more that you are demanding to do: "You lack one thing; go, sell what you have, and give it to the poor, and you will have treasure in heaven; and come, follow me" (Mark 10:21).

Jesus here assumes the authority of God. The young man realizes that he is face to face with more than just another "Good Teacher." Jesus makes claims that only God can make; here, He even amends everything that has been understood about God's demands.

The rich young ruler can no longer escape into his little hideaway of intellectual difficulties. The command is blunt and straightforward; he cannot possibly misunderstand: he must burn his bridges behind him and join Jesus. To make absolutely sure that there will be no retreat, he is ordered to get rid of his possessions.

". . . sell what you have. . . ." Our man gets red in the

face and sputters that this is preposterous! He can't do *that!* There are many reasons why he cannot give everything away, and all of them are sound. Why, if he and everybody else were to sell all they had and give it to the poor, it would wreck the economy. What kind of a nutty scheme is that? It would throw him on the relief rolls, and there are enough people in poverty row already. How is he supposed to manage? The sort of nonsense Jesus is suggesting is sheer idiocy; it means that he would be shirking his responsibilities. No, Jesus is making unreasonable, impossible demands. The rich young ruler turns away.

As he does, he thinks, "If only He had asked me anything else. Why, I would have read some books, or gone to worship services regularly, or made a decent pledge to the church, or agreed to get busy in church activities. But giving everything away! How does He think He can demand all this? Who does He think He is, anyhow?" Disappointed, the young man starts to walk away.

Jesus does not run after him. We might expect Jesus to pause, then call, "Hey, wait a minute! You didn't quite understand Me. Don't go away. Let's talk it over some more." After all, this man would be quite a disciple. He'd give Jesus' cause a real boost. It would be an asset to add this man as a convert; it would give status to Jesus, improve the image of Jesus' followers. Where is Jesus' sense of good public relations? Here He is allowing a local big shot, a man of wealth and power and prestige, to slip through His fingers. Surely Jesus can reconsider in this man's case. Can't Jesus lower the admission requirements slightly?

Jesus says nothing. The answer to the young fellow's problem is Jesus Himself. Refusing to go along with the man's attempt to have a friendly, stimulating interplay of thoughts with a "Good Teacher," Jesus has made him encounter God. He has called him to follow and have fellowship with Him. The young man walks away from the invitation. Surely, there are no more sorrowful words in the New Testament than: ". . . and he went away . . ." (Mark 10:22).

There is no bargain-counter discipleship with Jesus, and He will not offer anyone salvation at a discount. Instead of lowering the requirements for this man, He raises them. Jesus offers no enticements or "come-ons" to anyone; missing entirely are the gimmicks and "conversion techniques." Jesus lays it on the line: there is a new life with Him, but it comes only after a decisive break with the past. This costs, this hurts. Jesus bluntly asks, "Are you prepared to sacrifice —everything?"

Jesus is not laying down any universal law for discipleship. Some people misconstrue the story of the rich young ruler to mean that every follower of Jesus is to embrace total poverty. Jesus, like a skillful Physician, prescribes the necessary medicine for each individual's health. In the case of this man, it meant the radical surgery of cutting away his possessions. His bank book was standing between himself and God. Discipleship was the desired end; for this particular man, poverty would have been a necessary means to that end.

The rich young ruler wanted the best of both worlds. Faith must be painless, he insisted. Like us, too often he tried to have a relationship with Jesus without a cross. Without tears, without sacrifice, we are really not in earnest about Jesus Christ. Giving little, we wonder why Jesus means so little, or why we "get so little out of the Bible," or why worship "doesn't seem to do anything" for us.

In 1900, Sir Ernest Shackleton, the Arctic explorer, put an advertisement in the *London Times.* It read: "Men wanted for hazardous journey. Small wages. Bitter cold, long months of complete darkness, constant danger, safe return doubtful. Honor and recognition in case of success."

This could be an ad for Christianity. Jesus did not come

to offer an armchair, slippers, and tranquilizers. Rather, He holds out a cross and calls us to a life of sacrifice.

In our statistics-minded church structure, it is important to remember that Jesus had at least one failure: the young ruler was one man whom He never converted. "My church is the cheapest club I belong to," a man laughed. We the church like to be "accepted," so we let anyone "in." Have we forgotten that the words "discipline" and "discipleship" are closely related? Too often we the church whistle at the rich young rulers and call, "Wait! We don't really mean it! It won't actually cost you or hurt you to serve our Master." Jesus meanwhile puts every follower to the test: "Are you prepared to give up even your favorite interests, hobbies, toys, possessions, associates—*whatever* you may hold to be most important—for My sake? Are you holding back?"

After this breathtaking question comes the climax of the interview with you or me or any rich young ruler. "Follow me," Jesus says. Here is the highest requirement of all: personal allegiance to your personal Saviour. The call of Jesus is more than a call to turn your back on the past, and more than a call to sacrifice. More than anything, it is a call for fellowship with Him "whom to know is life, whom to serve is freedom, whom to love is joy," as the ancient prayer says.

There is a postscript tacked on each of the three gospel accounts of the interview with the rich young ruler. Our prosperous young man pads away slowly, shaking his head wistfully, and we hear no more of him. The disciples of Jesus, however, are open-mouthed. They think that success is a sign of piety. How is it that a respected, well-to-do man has failed to impress Jesus? Aware of their thoughts, Jesus tells them how hard it is for a rich man to enter the Kingdom. Using an illustration of a camel trying to squeeze through a needle's eye, He states that it is even less likely that a rich young ruler can squeeze into the Kingdom.

"Then who can be saved?" someone blurts (Mark 10:26).

No one; not one person can be saved by being successful or by being clever. No one can be saved by being powerful, prosperous, or respectable. No man can ever be saved by being sober, decent, or upright; by being industrious and thrifty; or by being religious; or by being well-read and intelligent. You are not saved by anything you try to do to "earn" His forgiveness and fellowship. "With men it is impossible," He states unequivocally. But He adds, "but . . . all things are possible with God" (Mark 10:27).

And through Jesus Christ, God has done the "impossible": He has accepted *you.*

7

The Woman of Samaria

THEY HAD been walking all morning and the well looked like a good stopping-place for lunch. Jesus sat on the low wall of the well while the disciples went to a nearby village to buy provisions. Hot, tired, and thirsty, Jesus wished for a refreshing drink from the well. Note that Jesus was as human as any of us: He knew what it was to be parched from thirst and to long for water. Note also that Jesus did not rustle up any "miracle" for Himself; He waited, as any of us might have waited, for somebody to come along with a leather bucket on a long rope and offer Him a drink.

Finally, there were footsteps on the path. Surprisingly, it was a woman who approached. It was very unusual for a woman to come to the well at noon, the hottest part of the day, the time when everyone preferred to stay in the shade. Even today, in the Middle East the women always fill their water jars in the early morning and at sunset, the cooler parts of the day. The village nearest to the well was a half mile away. No sensible woman would have walked a half mile and back in the height of the heat, carrying a heavy water jar. Furthermore, filling the water jars was—and still is—a sort of social event and gabfest. The women linger at the well, visiting and chatting, taking a break from their housework. Anyone coming to the well at noon was obviously trying to avoid meeting other people, especially other women.

Jesus sensed immediately that there was something peculiar about this woman. She apparently had been ostracized by the other women, and deliberately came to fill her water jar when none of them were around.

Jesus does a surprising thing: He speaks to the Samaritan woman, asking her for a drink. In speaking to her, Jesus smashed three long-standing barriers. First, He spoke to a woman; second, a Samaritan woman; third, a Samaritan woman of unsavory character.

Jesus completely broke with convention in speaking to a woman in the first place. No self-respecting man ever spoke to a woman in public. In fact, a man did not even address his own wife or mother or sister in public because women were considered so inferior to men. It was considered especially unfitting for a rabbi to speak to a woman in public.

He broke a second deeply-established tradition. There had been a long-standing antagonism between Jews and Samaritans. Jews looked down their noses with contempt and regarded Samaritans as compromisers. Samaritans, predictably, reacted by loathing all Jews, sometimes even resorting to violence. The feeling ran so high that Jews usually tried to avoid Samaritan territory by detouring many extra miles, even though the shortest distance between Galilee and Judea was through Samaria.

Jesus broke a third custom by addressing a woman with a shady reputation. Others would have turned away, pointedly snubbing her.

Jesus smashes all the barriers separating people. Our racial barriers separating whites and Negroes from one another, our class or social barriers, our religious barriers, our national barriers seem to be mile-high walls. In speaking with a woman, a Samaritan woman with loose morals, Jesus blasted the man-made partitions that keep us from understanding each other.

The Samaritan woman does a most unusual thing: she

parries in conversation with Jesus. Instead of silently handing Him the leather bucket, she gets a bit fresh and twits Him for asking her, a Samaritan, for a drink. She can tell that the tired Stranger is a Jew by the tassels on His robe; she relishes the idea that she can make Him squirm, and enjoys teasing Him. The fact that a woman speaks to a strange man means that she is plainly and openly flirting.

Jesus, of course, does not go along with her banter. "If you knew . . . ," He says soberly, "who it is that is saying to you, 'Give me a drink,' you would have asked him, and he would have given you living water" (John 4:10).

Living water has a double meaning. One meaning, of course, is plain, ordinary, drinking water. The other meaning, common to everybody in those days, refers to God. "My soul thirsteth for God, for the living God," the psalmist wrote (42:2, KJV). There are frequent references to God throughout the Bible as the One who satisfies the deepest needs of a person, as only fresh water will satisfy a parched, perishing desert traveler. Thus Isaiah cried, "Ho, everyone that thirsteth, come ye to the waters . . ." (55:1, KJV).

The Samaritan woman is still impudent with Jesus. There is a note of sarcasm as she asks just who does He think He is with all His fine talk of "living water"—Someone greater than Jacob? How is He going to get a drink, if He thinks He is so great?

Yes, He is greater than Jacob. Making it clear that He is not talking about water from that well which Jacob dug, Jesus points out again that He has the "living water," the meaning of life, to offer her. With short, quick wordstrokes, He paints a picture of what it means to know Him. Living for anything else in life except Him, he says in effect, is like trying to quench one's thirst at a salty, brackish reservoir. The contents of this tank are stale, stagnant, and eventually exhausted. On the other hand, living for Him is like being beside a deep artesian well gushing inexhaustibly with life-giving refreshment.

Jesus' words are lost on the woman. It is hard to tell whether she is thick-headed or simply determined not to listen to Jesus and understand the higher meaning to His words. Whether she is dense or stubborn or both, she clearly is thinking only of mere human thirst. She will not thirst? She won't have to carry this water jar again? What kind of a labor-saver is this Stranger talking about?

She gives a coarse laugh and tells Jesus to give her some of this water so that she won't have to trudge out to the well twice a day with a heavy jug. She wants to "use" Jesus like a modern convenience, like good plumbing, to bring running water.

How often we want to make Jesus fit our needs rather than allow ourselves to fit His needs. How often we regard God as a flunky. Too many of us think prayer is a gimmick to get what we want. Just as this woman tried to make Jesus a tool for getting her water, so we try to make God another gadget for comfortable living. God is not a labor-saving device. He will not serve our ends; He insists He will be real to us only when *we* serve *Him*.

The Samaritan woman wants to skirmish harmlessly with words. Jesus sizes her up: a shallow, flippant woman of loose morals. "Go," He commands abruptly, "call your husband . . ." (John 4:16). This is the touchy subject, the one sensitive area of her life. She stammers as she tries to rally her defenses, "I have no husband" (v. 17). Jesus is relentless; He stings her by pointing out that she has lived with some half dozen men, and the man she's currently living with is not married to her.

All her dirty little secrets are out. Jesus' words are like a glaring spotlight picking out the shame she has so carefully hidden in the shadows for so long.

But she tries to run away again. Even though Jesus has lanced her conscience, there is no penitence. She evades. She says to herself, "All right, this strange Man is a Prophet. Conceded. But He cannot go on exposing me as a cheap no-good. Get him off on a 'religious' topic. He's a Jew; I'm a Samaritan—I'll talk about the age-old squabble between Jews and Samaritans."

And she tries to sidetrack Jesus by raking up the hoary controversy over whether one could worship only on Mt. Zion, as the Jews claimed, or only on Mt. Gerizim, as the Samaritans claimed. This was always good for a couple of hours' heated debate between a Jew and a Samaritan. Jesus settles the ancient argument with a few words; He points out that because of Him the time has come when she does not have to go to Mt. Gerizim or Mt. Zion or any other special place to visit God.

In a sentence, Jesus devastates both the Jewish and the Samaritan arguments. Each had claimed that God could be localized; each had ties with a "good old mountain," like many people today who insist on keeping their church memberships back home in the "first church" even though they've been away for thirty years. "God always seemed closer back in Good Old First," they say, just as their counterparts said, "God always is closer on Gerizim," or "God is nearer on Zion."

Jesus demolishes the notion that tradition is all-important, as both Samaritan and Jew had claimed. Each of their arguments ran: "Our fathers worshiped there—if it was good enough for them, it's good enough for us." Venerating the past, like so many of us, they made custom their deity.

A new day has dawned with Jesus Christ. Our out-worn loyalties and petty loyalties as Jew or Samaritan are now meaningless.

It is always interesting to "talk about religion," but Jesus sees the topic for what it usually is—a dodge, an evasion.

Such talk simply raises minor questions and ignores the major one: Are you in the right relationship with God? Jesus has one purpose: He wants the Samaritan woman to know Him as the real God and to respond to Him with a radical change.

The Samaritan woman has tried unsuccessfully to divert the conversation. Like others whose knowledge is limited to what divides various faiths, she knows only old shopworn arguments against someone else's beliefs. But she tries to switch the dial to still another channel of conversation. This time she tries to get Jesus on the "safe" topic of the Messiah. Everybody, Samaritans and Jews, looked for a Deliverer and talked about His coming.

Jesus has had enough of her evasions. He openly announces that He is the Messiah.

The woman jumps up and runs to her village, and in her excitement she leaves behind her water jar. There are now more important things to attend to than filling water jars. Her words to the villagers are reminiscent of the first fishermen-disciples: "Come, see . . . ," (John 4:29). The impetuous woman brings the entire village on the run to the well.

Until this moment, she has been an outcast, shunned and shunning. With her staggering announcement, however, she forgets her shame. Instead of avoiding people, as she had been doing, she now hunts them out. The woman of Samaria is one of the first to learn that knowing Jesus means that the barriers between you and others are removed. The Samaritan woman is also aware that knowing the Good News of Jesus Christ means sharing it.

They tell the story in the northwest about a boy who had been active in his church and who went off to work in a logging camp. Everyone knew how rough the loggers were, and wondered how the boy as a Christian would be able to stand up under their jibes and teasing. Would he remain loyal to the faith? Everyone waited anxiously for his return. When he came back months later, people crowded around him in the church to ask if he had withstood the taunts of the loggers. The boy avowed that he had. His friends were pleased and asked how he had kept his faith. "Well," he answered, "no one ever found out about it."

This is all too typical of us who receive the Good News. The Samaritan woman, for all her deficiencies, at least reacted by telling others about the meaning of the Stranger she encountered in the midst of the daily routine. Being a hearer of the Good News means becoming a missionary.

Seventy-some years ago, a young teacher in Alabama held her little blind, deaf pupil's hand under the stream flowing from a pump spout and manually spelled out the word "water." The teacher's name was Anne Sullivan; the little girl's, Helen Keller. As a surprise for Miss Keller, her grateful classmates at Radcliffe College presented a lovely fountain to the college on their fiftieth class reunion. The fountain is called the Anne Sullivan Memorial Fountain. Before feeling the water, Miss Keller read a Braille inscription on the back of the fountain: "In memory of Anne Sullivan, teacher extraordinary, who beginning with the word, water, opened to the girl Helen Keller the world of sight and sound through touch."

Undoubtedly, that woman of Samaria returned often to the well of Sychar where she had first encountered Him who is the living Water. If she could have erected a plaque, the inscription might have been something along the same lines as the tribute to Anne Sullivan: "Jesus Christ, Teacher extraordinary, who beginning with the word, water, opened to the woman of Samaria the whole world of purpose and forgiveness through Himself."

8

Peter, James, and John

YEARS AGO our Sunday school pictures showed Jesus as such a delicate, dainty Person that one boy commented that He looked like Mary Pickford! We boys had no desire to learn anything about an ineffective, docile Jesus. Most of the people who seemed interested in Him were tame, tired, elderly women. One of these women kept telling us that Jesus wanted us to be little sunbeams for Him. We didn't want to be sunbeams for Jesus; we wanted to be locomotive engineers and cowboys. For us, there was little that was exciting or interesting about Jesus. We were made to listen to sugary poems about Him—pious drivel describing a benign Dreamer on quiet little nature walks.

No wonder so many of us grew up thinking Jesus is dull, tame, and colorless! No wonder the poet Swinburne wrote off Jesus as "that pale Galilean." No wonder a college student wrote to his pastor asking to be dropped from the rolls of the church, explaining that he had "outgrown" Christianity because "Jesus Christ was so innocuous and irrelevant."

Dull, tame, and colorless? Pale Galilean? Innocuous and irrelevant? Far from it! Proof? Take a look at the group of men He attracted as followers, especially the three who were an inner circle of the Twelve: Peter, James, and John.

If your mental image of these three is that of a trio of serene old men with limp hands, erase it. Color them in bold, positive, violent tones, not pale pastels. They were bold, positive, violent men. Jesus dubbed them with nicknames that leave little doubt about their personalities. Simon was nicknamed "Peter," which is best translated as "Rocky"; the brothers James and John were called "sons of thunder." Men who were familiarly known as "Rocky" and "sons of thunder" would hardly have had much to do with a milk-and-water Jesus.

Peter, James, and John—the names recur so frequently in this sequence in the gospels that it is obvious even to the casual reader that these three were a tightly-knit trio within the disciple band. Probably they were boyhood chums who had played together, then worked together. Luke, in his account, specifically states that the three were partners in the fishing boats on Galilee.

When Jesus calls anyone to follow Him, He is not inviting him to a picnic in the park. "Follow me and I will make you become fishers of men," He bluntly told Peter, James, and John (Mark 1:17). Remember that these men were professional fishermen who knew what danger, risks, and fatigue meant. We who are summer-vacation fishermen think of fishing in terms of dawdling in a boat or relaxing on a river bank, spending a lazy, drowsy afternoon with a pole and a can of worms, Tom Sawyer style. Peter, James, and John clearly understood that Jesus summoned them to serious business, hard work, and possible death.

This threesome was special to Jesus. Perhaps it was because they and Andrew were the first four of the Twelve to be chosen. Perhaps it was because they were more dependable. Perhaps it was because Jesus had known them longer than any of the others. In any event, Jesus held them in particular esteem. Peter, James, and John were with Jesus most of the time; a close reading of the gospels hints that the other disciples came and went, except of course for the Jewish festivals and the last weeks of Jesus' life.

The three were present when Jesus healed Peter's

mother-in-law. By special invitation, they were the only ones present, besides Jairus and his wife, when Jesus brought Jairus' little girl back to life.

All twelve of the disciples wondered who Jesus was. The more they knew Him, the more they had to revise upward their estimate of Him. Peter, James, and John, thrown into closer contact with Jesus than the others, did more thinking about the meaning of Jesus' life.

Who was this Jesus, anyhow? Peter, James, and John probably discussed it among themselves. One day, near a village on the northern boundary of Galilee, Caesarea Philippi, Jesus cross-examined the Twelve on the subject. Eleven gave halting, tentative opinions. Peter blurted out the only conclusion that he could find: Jesus was the Messiah, the long-promised Deliverer. It seemed as if Peter had wanted to avow this for some time, but had been afraid to mention it publicly. Had he and James and John talked about Jesus as the God-sent Anointed One, and did Peter speak for James and John as well as for himself?

Peter's words were like a brilliant warming burst of sunlight on the minds of the others. Suddenly, they all had insight into who Jesus was, and they were delighted and relieved to have their big question answered.

Jesus' next words, however, were like a sleet storm; He predicted that He would be rejected and would suffer death and disgrace. The disciples were shocked. This was completely the opposite of all that they had understood about the Messiah. Their mental image of the Deliverer was a God-sent strongman whipping up enthusiasm among the masses; a popular hero leading the chosen people to victory over the hated enemies; a genial, capable ruler bringing perpetual peace and plenty. Jesus' prediction of His death rocked the beliefs they had been taught at their mothers' knees; it upset the cherished notions every good Jew held. Despised, rejected, suffering, and killed? What kind of

Messiah was He? Who was this Jesus whom they lived with and thought they knew so well? What were they in for?

Peter fussed and blustered that Jesus couldn't possibly mean what He had said. Jesus sternly silenced him: "Get thee behind me, Satan . . ." (Mark 8:33, KJV). Peter, James, John, and the others were wobbly, uncertain, groping, afraid.

Jesus once took Peter, James, and John away for about a week. They hiked north and stayed on the mighty slopes of Mt. Hermon in complete solitude. What followed will always remain shrouded in mystery; we cannot "explain" what took place. The essentials of this episode are that God disclosed a tremendous truth, and this disclosure was so immensely significant that it transformed the thinking of the three disciples. Some people try to "explain" the awe and mystery of the transfiguration by giving plausible reasons for the details, such as insisting that the men were dazzled by the light on the snow, or that they were simply dead-tired and had a dream, or that the entire episode is a misplaced account of the resurrection, or that it is a myth. These are attempts to make rational and reasonable what the participants never claimed was rational or reasonable. They were totally unconcerned about the external details. They knew only that they had been given insight into the meaning of Jesus Christ. We are talking about the inner experience of Peter, James, and John; it is impossible to be objective about something that is subjective.

The recorded details are loaded with meaning. ". . . a cloud overshadowed them," the gospel writer states (Mark 9:7). In Jewish thought, God's presence was symbolized by a cloud, as when Moses met God (Exodus 16:10; 19:9; 33:9), or when the Temple was dedicated (I Kings 8:10). When it was said that a cloud came down, every Jew knew that this was the same as saying that God Himself was present.

Peter, James, and John no longer had the same idea of Jesus after their experience on Mt. Hermon. Jesus was not the same Companion they had walked with, eaten with, talked with so often; they saw Him in a different light. Even His face and peasant robe seemed to radiate a quality that marked Him apart from others. They were aware of a divine energy in Jesus.

The account of the transfiguration demands to be sung rather than read. It is not prose; it is a chorale of faith. Interesting side-themes appear as the account moves toward the mighty crescendo: "This is my beloved Son; listen to him" (Mark 9:7). One interesting side-theme is the reference to Moses and Elijah. Moses and Elijah were indisputably the two greatest men of all time to Peter, James, and John, who were good Jews. God had spoken through Moses, the great lawgiver, and He had spoken through Elijah, the great prophet. Yet these, great as they were, faded in the light of Jesus Christ. Peter, James, and John were given to understand that Jesus surpassed even Moses and Elijah, that Jesus summed up the law and the prophets. Jesus was God's Son, His Chosen.

Because they understood the real meaning of His ministry, Jesus seemed to rely on Peter, James, and John even more. During the remainder of Jesus' life, they were His trouble shooters, His special messengers, His closest associates. However, they must have made Jesus want to cry with disappointment on many occasions. Disgustingly human, they often behaved as if they had never been on the mountain at the transfiguration.

For example, once James and John were so irritated by the lack of hospitality of a group of Samaritans that they stomped up to Jesus and, steaming with rage, demanded that He rain down fire and wipe out the entire village. Or, there was the occasion when James and John were so childishly ambitious and selfish that they allowed their mother to appeal to Jesus for the Number One and Number Two seats in the Kingdom for them. Again, there was big-mouthed talk by Peter and his shameful denial at the trial of Jesus. None of this threesome ever consistently fulfilled Jesus' hopes for him.

And yet Jesus wanted them near. He enjoyed their companionship; they continued to be the inner circle. Often, while conversing with them He clarified what no one had quite understood.

There was, for instance, the occasion when He had commented on the coming destruction of the Temple. All of the disciples had been puzzled; Peter, James, and John came to Jesus and asked Him to elaborate. Jesus told them that the political situation was so bad in Palestine that a blowup was inevitable, and that when it came, look out! conditions for His followers would be too horrible to describe. Peter, James, and John were the privileged conversationalists with the Master.

During the last days before the crucifixion, Jesus seemed to depend on these three even more. He asked two of them, Peter and John, to make the arrangements in the upper room for the Last Supper. Finally, in Gethsemane, in the closing hours of the drama, He leaned on Peter, James, and John as never before.

The transfiguration had been a momentous occasion in the life of Jesus. Peter, James, and John had shared it and had understood it. Jesus now faced the unsettling time of questioning and anguish, and He again wanted His most intimate associates to stand with Him. Although all the disciples except Judas were in Gethsemane, Jesus specifically requested this group of three reliables, with whom He had been through so much, to sweat it out with Him.

It was an intense struggle for Jesus. Time was running out and it was the last night He would be alive on earth. The final showdown was only hours away; Judas had turned traitor, and would soon be coming with the Temple police. The disciples were shaky. Dull-witted, sleepy-eyed clods, they were poor material to build on. By human standards, Jesus' cause was failing. There was so much left unsaid and undone. He knew He would soon be executed, unless—unless some changes were made quickly. Jesus was tempted as He had never before been tempted. Was there no way of pulling things together to avoid the cross?

Jesus was no ascetic, no Hindu-type holy Man who renounced everyday life. He enjoyed life; He had no wish to escape it, no desire to die. Did He have to suffer for others? Did He have to lay down His life for such fickle, blind, stupid, selfish fools as even His disciples were? Was there no way less costly than a cross? Did He have to walk that grim road up to Calvary?

Talk about anguish, no one ever knew struggle as intense as Jesus went through. Torn between His human and divine feelings, He drew upon all the physical and emotional reserves He had. The Greek words in the gospel account (Mark 14:34) could be translated, "This struggle is crushing the very life out of Me." In His mind, Jesus saw a cup of sorrow and suffering held out toward Him to take and drink, and He asked God if that cup could not possibly pass.

Where were the three closest friends, Peter, James, and John, during Jesus' agony? Praying with Him and for Him? Standing beside Him as He knelt, comforting and strengthening Him by their presence? No, they dropped off to sleep.

Alone, terribly alone, Jesus won the victory in Gethsemane. He chose submission to the Father's will instead of "success"; sacrifice instead of "security"; suffering instead of "superiority." He won this victory not only for Himself, but for Peter, James, and John—and all of us.

The question of whether or not we live for success, security, or superiority has been settled once and for all. Gethsemane, the cross, and the resurrection are God's emphatic answer.

Samuel Eliot Morison's *Victory in the Pacific* is a careful study of World War II in the Far East. Writing about one part of the costly struggle, Morison (who won seven battle stars, the Legion of Merit with combat clasp, and sailed in eleven ships) says simply, "For us who were there, or whose friends were there, Guadalcanal is not a name but an emotion."

For those who were in Gethsemane, or at Calvary, or by the empty tomb, or on the Emmaus Road, these were not simply names or places; each was an emotion. Peter, James, and John were profoundly affected by these mighty events; so much so, that they were present, still together, in the upper room after the resurrection. Later, the Apostle Paul wrote of knowing this triumvirate as the mainstay of the struggling, suffering but gloriously confident group of Christians in Jerusalem.

The first of the Twelve to drink the cup of suffering Jesus had promised was one of this threesome, James. The twelfth chapter of Acts states bleakly, ". . . Herod the king laid violent hands upon some who belonged to the church. He killed James the brother of John with the sword . . ." (vv. 1-2).

Peter and John, the survivors of the closely-knit group, fearlessly continued their witness to Jesus Christ. Threatened, imprisoned, tortured, they were steadfast. It is almost a certainty that they, like James, suffered martyrdom. Their preaching, writing, and living had only one purpose: ". . . that you may believe that Jesus is the Christ, the Son of God, and that believing you may have life in his name" (John 20:31).

9

The Gadarene Demoniac

THE SCENE was eerie enough to unnerve the most hardened: a weirdly overcast night following a storm; a wild stretch of cliff coastline pock-marked with open tombs and graves; a violent, screaming maniac on the loose.

Jesus, however, did not turn back. After near-disaster in the boat during one of Galilee's meanest rampages, Jesus and the men with Him wanted to rest for the remainder of the night. They landed in the darkness under the cliffs of a section of shoreline that is grim even in daylight. In those days, it was avoided for other reasons: it was a Greek-speaking area, the section of Palestine called the Decapolis, or "ten cities," colonized by corrupt, pagan outsiders. Respectable Jews had as little contact with the people of the Decapolis as possible.

This wild strip of coast was doubly polluted: it was a sprawling cemetery and a grazing area for an immense herd of swine. Jews were strictly forbidden to have anything to do with either tombs or pigs. Anyone landing on this shore was entering a contaminated area. Only an emergency drove fishermen like Jesus' friends to beach their boat there.

Blood-chilling shrieks pierced the night. A wild man of fantastic strength roamed the cliffs, often stumbling in his frenzy over the rocks, snatching sleep in the cave-tombs amidst the human bones. There had been attempts to capture him, but he was too strong for any one man to handle.

He had such superhuman power that he even broke apart chains. Repulsive and naked, he was allowed to scream and rave in this desolate sector where he could do little harm. No man wanted to cross the unpredictable maniac's path.

When the wailing man lunged at Jesus and His friends out of the dark, it must have been a terrifying experience. There was no fear, however, in Jesus. Instead of sprinting back to the boat, He advanced calmly and spoke. Jesus was taking His life in His hands to approach this dangerous man.

"Come out of the man, you unclean spirit!" Jesus commanded (Mark 5:8). "Unclean spirit" was the common term in those days for ailments of any sort, emotional or physical. Some thought that there was seven and one-half million evil spirits infesting the world, waiting to work harm on a person. Jesus was not being superstitious; He was simply using the commonplace words, just as we might speak of "germs" or "bugs."

Jesus quickly discovered that the man was a particularly stubborn case to heal. Instead of being calmed, the man wailed, "What have you to do with me? . . . do not torment me" (v. 7). Obviously, many others had tried to "help" him, usually with clubs and chains. In his fright and excitement, the deranged man thought Jesus and His friends were another crew who came to pick on him and hurt him.

Jesus was unlike others; He gave no orders to henchmen to surround the wild man. Instead, He quietly spoke, "What is your name?" (v. 9).

Jesus treated the man as a member of society, not as a "case." As Emerson once pointed out, Jesus was "the one soul in history who has appreciated the worth of a man." Jesus saw possibilities even in the maniac. The great artist Maxfield Parrish used to amuse his classmates at Haverford College by turning inkblots in their notebooks into interesting, lovely figures. Jesus saw this useless stain of a human being as one who could become a member of the community again. The man living in the tombs was in a sense "dead" already, but Jesus meant to resurrect him and send him back to life. Jesus was the first to treat the emotionally disturbed as human beings.

It has taken the church years to catch up with Jesus. Chained or caged like animals, the mentally ill were objects of ridicule, punishment, and embarrassment for centuries. It was only in the nineteenth century that a gentle but courageous Christian woman named Elizabeth Fry shocked the world by visiting the reeking dungeons of England, then called "madhouses." Spurred by Elizabeth Fry, Quakers in England and America opened the first hospitals for the emotionally ill. Since then, society has gradually learned to have concern for the one out of twelve persons who needs psychiatric hospital care. Elizabeth Fry's concern and society's concern stem from the concern originally expressed by Jesus. His ministry is the basis for our ministry to disturbed people.

"What is your name?" Jesus asked. In the ancient world, names were carefully guarded. If someone knew your name it was believed to give him control over you. Your name equaled your power; giving your name meant yielding your power to the authority of another. Names were kept carefully secret from strangers. For example, God's name, "I am," among Jews was never repeated aloud but was meticulously kept private. "What is your name?" was Jesus' way of asking the disturbed man to trust Him and to share something very confidential with Him.

The man was willing to acknowledge the authority of Jesus. He gave his name; in other words, he agreed that Jesus should have power over him.

"My name," the man answered, "is Legion" (v. 9). What an odd name. A legion was a Roman army unit of six thousand well-trained, highly-armed men. Perhaps this man was the unfortunate victim of some atrocity by a Roman legion. Hated by the population, the very word "legion" equaled death, terror, and destruction. Perhaps this demon-possessed man carried the emotional scars of a horrible encounter with some of Caesar's legionnaires.

There was a Jewish saying, "A legion of hurtful spirits is on the watch for men saying, 'When shall he fall into the hands of one of these things and be taken?'" Seething in the maniac was a host of horrible evil powers. Not only one or two, but entire regiments of demons were plaguing this man among the cliffs and tombs.

"My name is Legion; for we are many" (v. 9). Note the transition from the singular "my" to the plural "we." One man speaking, perhaps, but six thousand powerful voices within him were yelling; six thousand strong forces were tugging him apart. His reply revealed the terrible inner conflict of the man. Psychiatry can give a more precise clinical term but not a more vividly descriptive phrase for insanity than "My name is Legion; for we are many."

"Legion" is the illness plaguing us all. Too many voices, too many pressures, too many demands, too many interests screaming and struggling within us. "We are many," the conflicting interests within us shout. "We are many"—a conquering legion, armed and sent to trample and destroy.

"I don't know who I am," one perplexed man confessed recently. "I'm supposed to be a husband, a father, a salesman, an employee, a church member, a home owner, part of a veterans group, a Little League committeeman, an American, and a good guy to everybody. I'm each of these, and each is trying to tell me what I'm to do. I'm pulled this way and that. I'm confused and fed up. I honestly don't know who in the world I'm supposed to be. I'm fifteen or so different people."

This is typical of us all. We are walking collections of

pressure groups. We have too many names and we are not sure which ones to shed and which to keep. And even if we think we know which to leave, we are not able to chase away the other five thousand powerful forces of the legion which are trying to conquer us.

Jesus alone can bring order, unity, and purpose to our confused lives. Unless He is our Master, we are ripped and trampled by the six thousand masters raging within each of us.

In this account, as in many others in the Bible, the writer speaks of "demons" inhabiting a man. "Demons" sounds quaint and naïve. We are inclined to give our most sophisticated smile at this description and change the subject.

The point of this episode is that powerful forces had a grip on a man. Call these forces by any name you want: demons, as they did then, or paranoia, schizophrenia, psychosis, or complex, as we do now. By any name you want to use, you have to face the fact that the man's situation was desperate.

There are plenty of demons loose today—the demon of race prejudice is only one. The demon of guilt and the demon of anxiety are two more. We are "possessed," we say; and we are correct, for we *are* possessed by certain fears and prejudices. It is not enough to laugh and say that this is foolish. Much as we might want to be rational, we are not. We are hopelessly irrational when caught by guilt, anxiety, prejudice, or any of the other demons inhabiting us.

"Come on, pull yourself together," the world tells us. This is as pointless as telling a drowning man to swim. Pep talks and pat answers and advice are useless, even harmful. Obsessed with self as we are, we will not be saved by explanations and reasoning.

The powers of evil have a supernatural grip on us and the demons burrow deep into the dark places of our minds.

Even when we think they have gone away, we see their shadows marching across the screen of our subconscious thinking.

Christians have always claimed that we do not need an answer-man. Rather, we admit quite openly that we need a Saviour. Our human situation is desperate; "Deliver us from evil," we pray. We know too well the power of evil in our lives, and only a Deliverer can save us from it.

In Victor Hugo's *Ninety-Three*, a sailing ship is flailed by a heavy storm. Powerful seas and tremendous winds occupy everyone's attention. Then a thundering noise deep in the ship is heard. The crew blanch when they realize what has happened: a heavy gun has broken loose from its moorings and is careening wildly on a lower deck. It will be only a matter of minutes before the wheeled monster will hurl itself through the ship's side as the vessel rolls and pitches. Brave men must rush below to secure the huge cannon before it batters the ship apart. The real threat was within, not outside the ship.

So it is with us; the real threat is not the world around us. The real threat is not communism (dangerous though this is), or the economic situation, or social conditions, bad though any of these may be. The real threat lies within us. Powers of destruction are loose in each of us.

Jesus Christ delivers men from the powers of evil and destruction. No matter how tight the grip of the demonic forces raging within us, no matter how complete the ruin worked by the legion of demons in us, God is stronger. In His mighty act of deliverance through the life, death, and resurrection of Jesus Christ, He has absolutely and conclusively triumphed. The demons of guilt, fear, despair, prejudice—you name them—are not the reigning powers. God rules!

In the account of the meeting between the wild man of the tombs and Jesus, there is an odd detail that three gospel writers mention. It is such an unusual detail that no one could possibly have made it up. It is obviously something observed by eyewitnesses, and it adds authenticity to the account. It concerns a large herd of pigs nearby. As anyone who has ever been on a farm knows, pigs are easily stampeded. Somehow, this herd was made to panic and they galloped down to the precipice. Helpless to stop themselves, they tumbled over the rocks and, with unearthly shrieks that only pigs can make, splashed into the water below. This violent action is one more weird, dramatic touch to a night that was full of horrors.

Aldous Huxley, back in the nineteenth century, was one of the loudest to fuss over the destruction of these pigs. Even today, there are those who get sentimental about the death of some hogs, forgetting about the life of the demon-possessed man. Jesus was not heartlessly destroying livestock, as some have claimed. The main point of the story is that the dramatic stampede of the hogs was the means by which Jesus finally got through to this unhappy man. As the herd tumbled screaming over the cliff, it dramatized the power of Jesus to deliver a tormented man from the powers that had been ruining him. Jesus banished the demons which had seized him, not just temporarily, but once and for all.

Before we get hung up on the minor detail of the death of the hogs, let's remember what the popular idea was at that time. It was commonly assumed that demons could be permanently removed only by being cast into the sea. Everyone—participants, witnesses, writers in later times—knew that the man *was* cured. Water, to those people, meant the death of demons. Here was evidence that the demoniac had been healed.

Huxley and latter-day pig-lovers have not been the only ones to be more concerned about the price of pigs than the value of a man's life. There have been others with mixed-up sets of values. The first were the owners of the pigs and some of the villagers from the settlement of Gadara. They came dashing out in the early dawn after hearing about the events. They cared more about their swine than their neighbor, the demoniac.

What irony in that scene! There sat the man whom they had once hunted down and tried to chain, the frenzied maniac who had terrorized the district with his chilling screams and brute strength. For the first time in years, he was sitting, calmly and quietly, and wearing clothes. The villagers' reaction? Luke says, ". . . they were afraid" (8:25, KJV). They could accept a crazy man, frightening though he was; but they could not cope with a sane man with an idea. They were afraid of him.

It is typical of society. We can take a sick man better than we can a well man with a cause or an idea. The sick man can be locked up or put away. The well man, like the demoniac who had been given new life, is a threat.

We have heard so much meek-and-mild nonsense about Jesus that it surprises us to learn that there were actually people who brusquely asked Him to clear out of their area. This is exactly what the people of Gadara did. They did not see Jesus as any placid, harmless, bearded gent. He was a Disturber, and they resented him. "Depart from our neighborhood," they commanded.

Don't be surprised to find the same thing happening today. There will be violent reactions in your neighborhood when Jesus upsets the pattern of life. For example, try to be neighborly with a Negro who moves into an all-white suburb. You and he will be told in no uncertain terms, "Depart from our neighborhood." Any time you take a stand for Jesus Christ in your neighborhood, it will mean friction, tension, criticism, even name-calling and unpleasantness.

Whenever Jesus Christ does anything, He gets in the way

of some people. "Jesus is fine, as long as he doesn't interfere with our investments and our money," the pig-owners of Gadara said. "Just don't mix Jesus Christ with politics and business," many a "church"-man growls at his minister. Modern Gadarenes want to protect their vested interests. If Jesus is bad for business, then Jesus must go, they reason.

Down through history, the cry, "Depart from our neighborhood," has been heard because Jesus threatens someone's business or holdings. The Temple moneychangers and salesmen were furious when Jesus put them out of business one day during the height of the Passover season. So angry were they, that they wanted to have Jesus arrested on the spot.

The Apostle Paul enraged some businessmen who made their money from the malady of a slave girl who went into trances and told fortunes. When Paul healed the girl of her unhappy affliction, her owners were irate. They dragged Paul and Silas to court, accusing them of "disturbing our city." Paul and Silas were beaten and heaved into jail.

On another unforgettable occasion, Paul fomented a riot in Ephesus by preaching so effectively that trade in silver images of Artemis, patron goddess of the city, fell off sharply. Infuriated at this intrusion of Jesus Christ into business, the silversmiths went on a rampage against Paul and the other Christians.

Any time Jesus threatens the vested interests in any community, stand by for an outburst!

The Gadarenes, those who put business ahead of human need, are still very much with us. Take, for example, one of the most shameful aspects of present-day American life, the living conditions of migrant farm workers. The unskilled outcasts of a skilled economy, these migrants follow the crops northward in three circuits, from Florida to New York, from Texas through the midwest, from California through Washington. Some five hundred thousand migrant workers have no chance to vote, no effective unions, no minimum-wage protection, no unemployment insurance. Their average annual wage in 1958 was only $961. The principal victims of this national disgrace affecting forty-five states are children.

These children are usually full-fledged field-hands at the age of nine. When they come to a new area, school systems, often overcrowded already, wink at attendance laws. Falling behind, most migrant children quit school by the fourth grade. This group makes up the bulk of the illiterates in our country, and because of their handicaps these youngsters are condemned to take up the same hopeless lives as their parents.

For years, attempts have been made to pass laws providing for mandatory attendance of migrant workers' children at summer schools. Growers, however, have consistently opposed such legislation. Attempts to get local support for summer schools for migrant children have been complete failures. "If you make it too good for migrants, they'll stay," has been the reaction. When a bill was introduced in Congress providing for the federal government to pay up to seventy-five per cent of the extra cost of educating migrant children, it was hotly opposed by the farm lobbies. Explained one grower, "When a migrant goes to school beyond the seventh grade, you've ruined a good bean-picker."

The people of Gadara asked Jesus to leave their area, so Jesus and the handful of disciples walked down to their boat. The cured man begged to come with Jesus. Understandably, he wanted to remain with the Person who had brought him back from living among the dead, literally and figuratively. He also knew how difficult it would be to go back to where he was known.

Surely, we think, Jesus should have let him come along. What striking proof of Jesus' power he would have been!

He would have been a trophy, a prize exhibit back on the other side of Galilee. "Go home," Jesus told the man. "Tell them how much the Lord has done for you, and how He has had mercy on you."

Jesus sends us back to Pittsburgh, back to Middletown, back to Gadara, back to the job, back to our homes. We are sent to witness to God's mercy. This is the church at work in ministry.

We often mistakenly think that serving Jesus Christ means heading out on some romantic mission or an exciting adventure in a faraway place. Or, we think that responding to Jesus Christ means the stimulating fellowship of a theological seminary. To go to the farthest reaches of the earth as a Christian is in some ways easier than facing the old crowd, those who know us best, and witnessing to them. For most of us, the "foreign field" where Jesus Christ wants us to tell about Him is not a remote continent, but our offices, our factories, our kitchens.

Rudyard Kipling wrote a poem which vividly describes a fierce storm at sea during a voyage on board an old cattleboat. The lights go out on the lower deck and the cattle pens are smashed. The fear-stricken cattle stampede, and an irreligious, roughneck seaman named Mulholland is trapped. He knows that he is doomed to be gored or trampled to death by the herd rampaging through the dark on the pitching deck. At that moment, Mulholland decides to make a contract with God:

> If He got me to port alive I would exalt His Name,
> An' praise His Holy Majesty till further orders came.

Miraculously, Mulholland was spared, although he was badly injured and laid up in the hospital for seven weeks. When the time came to leave the hospital, he remembered his contract with God and thought with pleasure that he would not have to endure the existence in the filthy hold of a ship any longer. But then God surprised Mulholland:

> Back you go to the cattleboats an' preach My Gospel
> there.

Mulholland was flabbergasted. He replied,

> I didn't want to do it, for I knew what I should get;
> An' I wanted to preach Religion, handsome an' out of
> the wet;
> But the Word of the Lord were laid on me, an' I
> done what I was set.

We want to "preach religion, handsome an' out of the wet," but Jesus often sends us back to the hardest mission field of all—the place where we are known.

A locomotive engineer was so deeply moved one night while listening to the great Charles Spurgeon preach, that he came to see Spurgeon after the service, saying that he wanted to go into Christian work. Spurgeon asked the man if the fireman on his locomotive was converted. The engineer said that he was not. "My dear fellow," continued Spurgeon, "that is your piece of work."

The Gadarene who was healed was one of the early "home" missionaries. He was sent back to heal where he had hurt while under the power of demons. The folks in Gadara were the ones who needed him most.

Once, you and I were "possessed"; once, we were gripped by the demons of fear, guilt, and prejudice; once, you and I were people existing among the "tombs," living as people dead to God and dead to others. The wondrous news in Jesus Christ is that God has rescued us, healed us. His forgiving power puts us "in our right minds."

Your response? Take your miracle home with you!

10

Simon the Pharisee and the Repentant Woman

THE HOST'S name was Simon. Active in religious affairs, he was called Simon the Pharisee. He was anxious to get a line on Jesus; he had Him pegged as a Prophet of some sort, but wanted to look Him over more closely. Condescendingly, he asked Jesus to dinner and felt that Jesus should feel honored by such an invitation. After all, not everyone was privileged to sit at Simon's table. As a Pharisee, Simon enjoyed the respect due one who carefully cultivated an image of man who took his religion seriously.

Dinner parties at Simon's were always respectable. As was the custom, only men were present. Suddenly, there was a commotion at the door, and in burst a woman. This was extremely bad taste—a woman, uninvited, invading a men's dinner party. It was particularly shocking that it should happen in the home of a proper Pharisee. The real shock came an instant later when everyone recognized the intruder. She was a well-known streetwalker. Mouths flew open, for they knew what an unsavory reputation this local character had.

Before the aghast men, the woman made a spectacle of herself. She broke down and began to cry and sob. Then she disgraced herself further, doing something that was considered positively indecent: she undid her hair and let the tresses fall about her. No respectable woman would ever have been guilty of such immodest behavior.

Making matters worse, she reached inside the neck of her robe and brought out the expensive phial of perfume that every woman carried around her neck in those days. Still sobbing uncontrollably, she broke the costly bottle and poured its contents over Jesus. This was an act in such poor taste that the guests began to protest. Such an extravagance was just plain waste, several murmured.

The woman ignored them. Completely carried away, she knelt at Jesus' feet and cried her heart out, wiping His feet with her hair. Jesus sat calmly and made no move to stop her.

It was quite a scene, one that those present never forgot. Offended, Simon the Pharisee stood up. He was upset that his party was hopelessly wrecked. He was disgusted by the way the woman carried on. What annoyed him more than anything was that his Guest Jesus had not reacted in the proper manner. What kind of a Prophet was Jesus, anyhow? Couldn't He detect what kind of a character the woman was? Even if He didn't know her background, how could He sit there and let her behave so disgracefully? All of the rules of etiquette dictated that Jesus should have recoiled in horror at being touched by such a loathsome creature. Simon was right; Jesus did not observe the social standards.

Jesus was always unpredictable. He persistently ignored the little norms and customs that society imposes upon itself. He did not care a rap if He shocked those of refined tastes such as the cultured, pious Simon. In His concern for people, Jesus associated with everyone. The first thing to notice in this episode is the fact that Jesus was involved not only with respectable "religious" people; He was even willing to be associated with a common streetwalker.

The next thing to note is that Jesus got through to the

woman. Well known in the area, she had been snickered at as a "floozy," ogled by teen-aged boys, given leering looks and obscene comments by young bachelors, spat at by housewives, used by half-drunken camel drivers. She had a coarse laugh and a lewd retort for everyone—except Jesus. The astounding thing is that such a tough, hardened "case" as this woman should have been affected by Jesus. He was able to do what few, if any, psychiatrists have been able to do with this kind of woman.

Jesus saw the woman as the person she actually was: someone who was lonely for God's presence, dying for want of His forgiveness. Simon the Pharisee saw her as a degraded object, as "just a prostitute."

Simon was annoyed that his Guest of Honor had missed the boat, and took it upon himself to tell Jesus all about her, pointing out her flaws and shame. (How typical of all of us! How often we think we have to tell God about the wickedness of everyone else!) Then Simon tried to direct Jesus. This woman was obviously a sinner, he told Jesus, and must not be allowed to touch anyone, but must be evicted immediately.

Simon had everyone neatly classified into two heaps: sinners and nonsinners. Needless to say, he assumed that he was in the small heap marked "nonsinners." Jesus, however, did not classify anyone. Jesus cares not so much what you are as He cares *who* you are. Abstract rules, rigid categories are just not in Jesus' thinking. He saw this woman not as a type but as a person. Simon's classifications really meant "unrespectable" (like her) and "respectable" (like him). Jesus flatly refused to make respectability the test of goodness.

It was Jesus' turn to be annoyed, and His irritation was directed not at the woman but at Simon the Pharisee. Jesus had had enough of Simon's gossip and preachments. Swiftly, with words that snapped, Jesus cut the Pharisee down to size. Even by Simon's own standards, Jesus told him, he had failed completely. Simon had not extended even the most elementary courtesies to his Guest. Jesus reminded Simon that even when it came down to being "respectable," Simon had not begun to live by his own standards. A respectable man would have washed a guest's feet; a respectable man would have extended a kiss of welcome; a respectable man would have anointed his guest's head. Simon had done none of these. Who did Simon think he was, Jesus implied, to strut so self-righteously and make such sweeping pronouncements about others? Respectability? Was this what Simon thought was the standard by which to judge everyone? So Jesus held Simon against his own yardstick and exposed him as the most unrespectable person in the room.

Simon the *Pharisee*—the "good" man—could not even come up to his own requirements of mere respectability. If he could not come up to a man's standards, how could he ever hope to come up to God's? Simon was spotlighted as one who was as far from being right with God as was the woman. Both the Pharisee and the prostitute were in need of God's forgiveness. Every one of us, we now know, stands before Jesus with the same label: "sinner."

We think "sin" means something as gross as prostitution. Jesus redefined "sin" to include pride and superiority. What we dismiss as mere examples of middle-class haughtiness are on a par with prostitution, according to Jesus. The sensual sins are not the only ones that separate men from God.

Jesus knew very well what kind of woman it was who had collapsed weeping at His feet; yet He did not dwell on the seamy details of her past or probe into her sordid personal history. There was no shrill denunciation. Others would have intoned, "Teach her a lesson!" or, "Make an example out of her so this won't happen to other girls!"

Concerned for the woman and not for "lessons" or "examples," Jesus did not condemn but forgave.

Do not ever think that Jesus was a sort of "forgiving machine," a robot clacking out assurance that people were forgiven. Some people have so cheapened the meaning of forgiveness that they imply it costs nothing, demands nothing. "God forgives," sneered the philosopher Heine one day after being reproved by his wife for his flippancy toward God, "God forgives, that's His business." There was no such attitude on the part of this one-time prostitute. Facing up to what she had been, she was ruthlessly honest with herself. Before Jesus, she knew she could no longer maintain any pretense. This woman realized what Simon the Pharisee did not realize: she had rebelled against God.

Jesus Christ can forgive only the person who will begin to be honest with himself as a sinner and honest with Jesus as Saviour. Until we face up to our moral bankruptcy, we are hopelessly lost.

The woman and the Pharisee are a study in contrasts. The Pharisee was on faultlessly good terms with himself. Self-satisfied, he was contemptuous of others and content with himself. His self-deceit was so enormous that he sincerely believed that he had done everything to please God. The woman, on the other hand, was a sinner and knew it and admitted it; she was forgiven. Simon the Pharisee was a sinner, but did not know it and would not admit it; he was not forgiven.

Looking all of the Pharisees—like us or like Simon—in the eye, Jesus says in effect, "Do you not understand that in spite of her sin-burdened life this streetwalker is nearer to God than *you?* Do you not realize that she has what you lack—real honesty and deep gratitude?"

We never really begin to understand the meaning of divine forgiveness. We casually comment, "Well, if forgiveness is free, why bother to be loving? What's the point of being good, if God loves us no matter what we do? Why not do as we please?" Who do we think we are? "Good" people? So "good" that God decides that we are worth saving? Nonsense! God saves us in spite of our being unloving and unlovable.

Before such mercy, we are bound to respond by showing mercy to others. Knowing God's concern for us through Jesus Christ, we can only show concern for His other children. We are not forgiven because we are loving; we love because we are forgiven.

To illustrate this point for Simon, Jesus told a story about two men who were flat broke. One man owed ten thousand, the other owed one hundred thousand. The debts of each were assumed by another. Who, Jesus asked Simon, would be the more grateful of these two? Simon could give only the obvious answer, and he understood the obvious point of the story.

The prostitute knew how much God had done, and she was grateful. She wanted to show love in return. The adjectives describing her are: generous, out-going, impulsive, humble. Those describing Simon are: stingy, withdrawn, calculating, self-important.

To the woman Jesus said, ". . . go in peace" (Luke 7:48). "Go *into* peace," the words literally mean, as if Jesus has opened the doors to a beautiful mansion, or thrown wide the gates to a gorgeous garden. "Go into peace" means that Jesus has let down the barrier so that we can now go and live a life of peace with God. After the loneliness, misery, and strife of trying to live apart from Him, He opens the door into a new life. For this woman and for us, this is a new country: the promised land where we are meant to live.

11

Mary, Martha, and Lazarus

EVERYONE NEEDS a family circle. We all need people among whom we can relax and be ourselves, people who don't mind if we take off our shoes or eat our peas with a knife. We all need the healing brought by understanding intimates. The gentle teasing and laughter around a table, the silences when no one feels compelled to entertain—these mean more to us than we realize.

Jesus was no different; He too needed a home. After the start of His ministry, He spent little time in Nazareth, partly because His ministry took Him elsewhere and partly because He must have felt unwelcome there. The nearest thing to a family circle that Jesus had during His ministry was with Mary, Martha, and Lazarus. Their home in Bethany was one of the few places where He could be away from curious stares and constant demands.

Mary, Martha, and Lazarus were refreshingly ordinary. Martha was the eldest. She ran the household and gave the orders. A practical, active person, Martha was the dynamo of the family. Mary, her sister, was the opposite. Easy-going and sensitive, Mary would have preferred writing poems to washing the pans.

Mary's and Martha's portraits snap into focus quickly, showing up in vivid tones. Lazarus, however, only gradually emerges as a personality. He seems to be painted with shades of gray in the picture the gospel writers give us.

Nonetheless, Jesus was not only fond of Lazarus but felt genuinely close to him.

Mary and Martha leaned on Jesus as on an older brother, and Jesus in turn depended on them for the warmth and companionship of a home. They are first introduced in the New Testament during a family-type festival, the Feast of Tabernacles. Jesus, as one of the family, was seated in the cool, arbor-covered courtyard. Martha was the only one not present in the relaxed circle. Work, for her, was a compulsion and she drove herself, hurrying and worrying, preparing a lavish meal. A few simple dishes would have been fine, especially since Jesus was practically a member of the family.

Inevitably, Martha grew tired and tense. She began to feel sorry for herself and resented her role. Then her eyes lighted on her sister. There sat Mary, calm and cool in the courtyard, taking her ease like a lady of leisure. Any woman can sympathize with Martha. What housewife has not been on the verge of a blowup after a long, hot afternoon in the kitchen? Irritated at seeing her sister taking it easy, Martha peevishly snapped at Mary and Jesus, "Lord, do you not care that my sister has left me to serve alone? Tell her then to help me" (Luke 10:40).

It was so childish. Instead of quietly and discreetly asking Mary for assistance if she needed it, Martha made a scene. Her words betrayed that her work had gotten the best of her: she could not even bring herself to use Mary's name but spoke of her with the impersonal words, "my sister."

Jesus knew where the blame lay. He did not dismiss Mary and send her back with Martha to the kitchen. Instead, knowing that Martha had taken on too much, He answered, "Martha, Martha, you are anxious and troubled about many things; one thing is needful. Mary has chosen the good portion . . ." (vv. 41-42).

Martha was too busy over too many things. The table arrangement and the finger bowls had come to absorb too much of her time and energy. She fussed over the frills, majored in minors.

"One thing is needful," is Jesus' word to any member of the cult of busy-ness. Do not allow the trivia of life to take over, Jesus is saying.

Jesus never belittled work. He did not ignore the fact that we have jobs and duties, that there are chores to be done. The drone who tries to excuse his indolence or laziness on the grounds of his commitment to Jesus, forgets that Jesus toiled in a carpentry shop and worked an exhausting schedule in His ministry. Jesus was the busiest, hardest-working Man in history.

Yet He was never irritable, never temperamental, never ill, never anxious or worried. "One thing is needful," namely, God. First place in our lives must go to Him. Our society, however, glorifies the Marthas. The Puritan virtues of industriousness and hard work have been made into a creed by many of us. God's first commandment, however, still stands: "Thou shalt have no other gods before me" (Exodus 20:3, KJV). The job is not our deity.

Too many of us show the Martha-like traits of fussiness, fault-finding, tantrums, and anxiety. Too often, these are dead giveaways that we have tried to make work a substitute for God. Being busy is no excuse for not trusting and serving Him.

In 1848 a foot-loose young Scot named James Marshall noticed something shiny in a stream beside a sawmill in the Sacramento Valley in California. Tests showed that the shiny pebbles were gold, and the news brought thousands of people to California. Hundreds made fortunes, but what about James Marshall? He was so busy here and there that he never got around to staking out a claim. He was always poor; in fact, he was on public relief for years. They found his body one day in the 1880's in a shack near the stream where he had first found gold. He was still poverty-stricken.

That's our danger—being so busy here and there, doing this and that, that we never know the riches of God's mercy. "Mary has chosen the good portion," Jesus reminded Martha. Mary had undoubtedly helped prepare the dinner too, but she knew that the most important part of the occasion was the time spent with Jesus.

During the last months of Jesus' ministry, there were fewer happy reunions with His friends at Bethany. Jesus had known opposition from the authorities throughout His career, but now He found them threatening His life. He of course was fully aware that a cross lay ahead, but He still had work to complete. Jesus knew that if He appeared again at Bethany, or any other place near Jerusalem, He would be arrested and executed.

One day a terse message came from Martha and Mary: ". . . he whom you love is ill" (John 11:3). It was easy to read into the staccato sentence that the sisters were desperate. Lazarus obviously was critically ill. This unexpected turn of events meant that Jesus had to shape up His plans quickly. If He answered the call for help from His beloved friends, it meant He would be back in the public eye again, and that meant inevitably a final showdown with the authorities. The disciples knew this too, and were dumbfounded when Jesus announced they would return to Judea. "Rabbi," they protested, "the Jews were but now seeking to stone you, and are you going there again?" (v. 8). Jesus, however, looked upon the summons from Bethany as an opportunity to complete His ministry. He told them that Lazarus had become ill "so that the Son of God may be glorified by means of it" (v. 4).

Lazarus was dead before they crossed the Jordan, but they learned of the fact as they approached Bethany. Martha met them and sorrow made her more abrupt than usual.

Her greeting was, ". . . if you had been here, my brother would not have died" (v. 21), and there was bitterness as well as trust in her words.

Sympathetically, Jesus assured her that Lazarus would rise again. Martha nodded mechanically, but it was obvious that she thought Jesus' words were simply platitudes. Martha clung to some shadowy hope for something after death, but all the pious words and interesting philosophies she had heard and repeated in the past meant nothing. Lazarus was dead. Listlessly, Martha mumbled something about Lazarus rising again in the resurrection at the last day, but neither her heart nor her mind were behind her words. Jesus then startled her with a staggering claim: "I am the resurrection and the life," He told her. ". . . he who believes in me, though he die, yet shall he live, and whoever lives and believes in me shall never die. Do you believe this?" (vv. 25-26).

Suddenly, all the words and platitudes about death were unnecessary to Martha. She saw that she could trust Jesus, and that trusting Him was really trusting God. "In my own Person," Jesus in effect said, "I am the explanation of life and death. I am stronger even than death itself! Trust in Me as a greater reality than death. I am the One to rely upon. I have the last word, even over death."

Martha in those moments saw Jesus in a new light. She had known Him as a close personal Friend and had thought she understood Him well. We often mistakenly think we know all about Jesus, but we never do. Even those of us who think we have been so close to Him have never completely understood the meaning of Jesus Christ. We constantly discover Him to be greater than all our previous superlatives.

Martha left Jesus and went to the house where Mary and their friends were going through the typical Middle East mourning custom of shrieking and wailing. Martha extricated her sister from the hysteria and brought her outside to Jesus. Still sobbing, Mary collapsed before Jesus.

Jesus was deeply moved and sympathized with these sisters in their grief. John sums up Jesus' feelings in a brief phrase, the shortest verse in the entire Bible as well as the most poignant, "Jesus wept" (v. 35). Our Saviour was no robot without feelings. God did not masquerade as a human being. Truly Man, as well as truly God, Jesus knew the unbearable loneliness of the death of a person He loved.

Mary blurted out the same words Martha had used, ". . . if you had been here, my brother would not have died" (v. 32). Obviously, the two sisters had repeated this to one another many times before Jesus had come.

Perhaps these sisters meant by their words that Lazarus would have repudiated the very idea of dying if Jesus had been there. Maybe they were saying that Lazarus lost his will to live and simply gave up. Nobody, not even Lazarus, could have died with Jesus nearby. There was an immense vitality about Jesus. In His presence, no one could easily yield to death. And this is also true today.

"I am the resurrection and the life," He said. By way of illustration, Jesus asked to be taken to the tomb where Lazarus' body had been laid. What followed was not intended to awe or impress or scare; it was simply a sign pointing to Jesus as the resurrection and the life.

It must be clearly understood that Lazarus was dead. He was not in a coma or trance. He had been in the sepulcher four days. The popular idea in Jewish circles was that the soul hovered for three days around the tomb, hoping to reanimate the corpse. It was customary for the family to visit the tomb during those three days in the event that the body was not dead. After that, decomposition set in rapidly and they gave up hope. Martha and Mary pointed out how hopeless it was to go to Lazarus' sepulcher.

What followed was the most sensational of Jesus' acts: He

raised Lazarus from death to life! This caused a tremendous stir throughout the area. Predictably, the authorities were enraged.

Some have wondered why Lazarus was not mentioned in the accounts of the following days of Jesus' life, His last before the crucifixion. Why wasn't Lazarus with Jesus? The reason is that the authorities were so incensed at the popular reaction to Jesus' raising of Lazarus that they plotted to have Lazarus murdered. Lazarus was forced to get out of the vicinity of Jerusalem.

There were no words from Lazarus, no record of his experiences or reactions. He was silent. There was not even any mention about whether he was surprised, pleased, or what, on being brought to life again. He left no account of what it is like to die or what it is like afterward.

This is a good indication that the story of the raising of Lazarus is true. A writer of fiction could hardly have resisted putting words in Lazarus' mouth, or giving breath-taking revelations. People have always been so curious about this subject that someone who cooked up a story about Jesus bringing a man back to life would not have shown the restraint the gospel writer showed. The episode of Lazarus' rising was told for only one reason: to illustrate that Jesus was and is the resurrection and the life. Any time we allow ourselves to be distracted from the Person of Jesus in this event, we miss the point entirely.

Lazarus eventually died and was buried again, this time permanently. We, like Lazarus, will eventually experience the fact of physical death. God does not promise us immunity from disease, old age, or accidents, and Jesus did not do away with dying. He did, however, cause the death of death.

Our sense of helplessness is so great that it is considered bad taste even to mention death. We go to incredible lengths to disguise it, using such euphemisms as "expired" or "passed on." We no longer go to a graveyard but to a "Garden of Memories." The words "ashes to ashes, dust to dust" are often discarded as being "too morbid." We fondle platitudes about "immortality" and murmur that "part of us never dies."

We think that the end of our individual lives is literally the end of history. Death is the final humiliation, the ultimate seal of failure. We say that in the midst of life we die. God answers, "In the midst of death you are raised to life!" Even though we will go through the experience of death, God gives us His Word that He can raise us to newness of life.

Perhaps you are bound in the shroud of fear or caught in the graveclothes of despair. Perhaps you are buried hopelessly in selfishness. God comes to you in the Person of Jesus Christ and calls you by name. Jesus calls you to life. When you trust in Him, you find that He is literally a return to life: ". . . he that believeth in me, though he were dead, yet shall he live" (John 11:25, KJV), He states. You will find this to be true. Though you may be a dead man because of your past, Jesus means to resurrect you and restore you to life.

So many Christians have known that Lazarus' experience is also their experience that through the years the raising of Lazarus has been a favorite subject in church art. Paintings, sculpture, and mosaics depicting Jesus and Lazarus date back even to the third century. Sometimes, small images of Lazarus were attached to the outside of tombs of Christians.

Surprisingly, however, nothing is known of the subsequent life of either Lazarus or his sisters, Martha and Mary. Even more remarkably, there are few legends about them. The most common story is that the authorities banished Lazarus, Martha, and Mary, setting them adrift in a leaky boat on the Mediterranean. According to the legend, the boat was blown across to Marseilles where the three landed and lived the rest of their lives. There is, of course, no historical basis whatsoever for any of this account.

Our attention must ultimately be focused not on the members of the family of Bethany but on Him who was their Guest. He wants to be ours as well. Knowing and serving Him is still the one thing that is needful.

12

The Man Born Blind

UNTIL RECENTLY, blind beggars were common sights in any city in the Middle East. Visitors were shocked by their numbers, annoyed by their aggressive insistence for handouts. On arriving, outsiders saw the swarms of blind beggars on the streets as repulsive curiosities; within a few days, however, they took no notice of them. The wretches were simply an unpleasant part of the scenery, objects to be ignored.

Jesus spent His entire lifetime in such surroundings. Everyone was used to blind beggars—except Jesus. The gospel writer John mentions that Jesus *saw* a blind beggar. (The verb in Greek makes it clear that Jesus really looked at him and did not accidentally glance his way.) Jesus never took anyone for granted, never dismissed anyone as an object. He took notice of a blind beggar, even though blind beggars were an everyday sight.

When the disciples noticed whom Jesus was looking at, they bubbled with questions. ". . . who sinned," they asked, "this man or his parents . . . ?" (John 9:2). The disciples reflected the popular view that anybody blind or ill was being punished by God for sin. Before them was an example. The disciples were anxious to discuss the juicy topic of "The Origin of Evil and the Problem of Suffering."

Jesus refused to treat the blind man as a subject for discussion. To Jesus, he was a man.

Stepping up to the beggar, Jesus did a surprising thing: He touched and worked on the man's eyes. Eye diseases in the East are gruesome sights. In Jesus' day, anyone who touched the festering, oozing scabs was polluted and made ceremonially "unclean," according to the strict Old Testament law. But human need for Jesus took priority over observing the niceties of religious etiquette. Jesus spat, made a paste of some dust, soothingly applied this mixture to the sores, and then told the man to wash in the pool of Siloam in the city.

This story is not told as an interesting medical case. The clinical details are beside the point. People sometimes try to make Jesus into a clever primitive medic, or describe Him as an expert in psychosomatic cures. Jesus was not an exhibitionist, nor did He play a doctor's role.

Far from trying to dazzle or entertain, Jesus made it clear that His healing was a "sign." A sign does not point to itself; it points to something or someone else. This sign—and a favorite word for "miracle" in the New Testament should be translated "sign"—points to the goodness of God as revealed to us in Jesus. The episode of Jesus healing the man born blind was more than a wonderful act of kindness whereby a beggar was given his sight. It was a sign pointing to Jesus, the Light of the world, who brought God's light of mercy into the darkness of this man's life and every person's life.

What darkness that man must have known! He had the added misery of other forms of darkness besides having to live in the world without his sight. There was the darkness of despair. Unwanted, he was edged to the fringe of society. He had long since learned how useless he was. Reduced to begging, he had had to give away every scrap of self-respect.

He had no hope of ever being an honorable, productive member of the community. Even his family wrote him off as a burden and a nuisance.

He lived in the darkness of guilt. The religious people said that he had sinned and that God was giving him what he had coming to him. The loneliness of being cut off from other people was severe, but the loneliness of separation from God deepened the darkness. This blind man had been told that he would never be right with God.

Perhaps he lived in the darkness of doubt. In his total blackness, did he ask questions about God? Did he wonder what kind of an ogre the Almighty was?

The good news was that God had come into this man's gloom and night. "I am the light of the world . . . ," Jesus announced (John 8:12). This word "light" that Jesus used for Himself may not mean much to us, but to His hearers that day it was a loaded word. The rabbis had taught that the name of the Messiah was "Light." Throughout the Old Testament, "Light" is a synonym for God. Here are just a few samples: "The Lord is my light and my salvation . . ." (Psalm 27:1); ". . . when I sit in darkness, the Lord will be a light to me" (Micah 7:8); ". . . by his light I walked through darkness . . ." (Job 29:3); ". . . the Lord will be your everlasting light . . ." (Isaiah 60:19).

Jesus was God come among us in our darkness. Note well that He did not say, "I am going to shed some light." He was not as other teachers or prophets. Buddha believed he had a beneficial teaching to offer men, but as far as he himself was concerned, he claimed only to be the rediscoverer of old and forgotten paths. He urged his followers not to think of him but to concentrate on his teachings. Confucius declared that as often as he walked three abreast with others, he was certain to find a teacher. He asked, "How dare I lay claim to holiness or love? A man of endless craving who never tires of teaching I might be called, but nothing more." Mohammed, with all his lofty claims, cried that unless God cast the cloak of mercy over him, there was no hope for him at all. Contrast these with Him who announced, "I am the light. . . ."

The man born blind obeyed Jesus and went and washed in the Pool of Siloam. He regained his sight.

We find Jesus keeps His word when we obey Him. We often whimper, "Prove it to me, then I will obey Him." God says, "Obey Me, then you will have it proved."

Once the blind beggar took Jesus seriously, he found himself under pressure. As soon as he appeared in public after being healed, he became the target for insults and threats.

When Jesus touches a person, He doesn't wrap him up for safekeeping and send him to a rest home; Jesus sends him immediately to the battleline of life.

The authorities were incensed that the healing had happened on the sabbath, breaking one of their precious little blue laws. Outraged, they grilled the man with one question after another. There was a nasty tone in their cross-examination as they tried to pressure him into saying something that could be used as evidence against Jesus.

Neither their threats nor their sneers cowed this man; he stuck to his story. The authorities even picked on the man's parents. The parents were so intimidated that they shied away from giving their son any support. The neighbors and bystanders were incredibly insensitive, discussing the blind man as they might have talked about a dog.

The investigators even cornered the man born blind a second time. This time, they got tough. The substance of their words: Denounce Jesus or suffer the consequences. Throughout the furor, however, this man was loyal to Jesus. In fact, the more loyal he was to Jesus, the more Jesus came to mean to him.

Earlier, the man born blind had been somewhat guarded about saying much about Jesus. He referred to "The man called Jesus . . ." (John 8:11). This is a good starting place, but the man soon found that he could not explain Jesus in terms of being simply a Man. The next time anybody asked him about Jesus, he tried to sum up what Jesus meant by stating, "He is a prophet" (v. 17). As the abuse and pressure increased, the man born blind was driven to think more about his Healer. Even the term "prophet" was not adequate. When the investigators surrounded him again, he boldly told them that the world had never seen anyone like Jesus.

Jesus is unique. The more we think on what He means, the greater He becomes. Step by step, the man once blind found his faith deepened. The more he knew about Jesus, the less he was intimidated by others. In the face of the sneers, the questions, the threats, the man stood firm with one conclusive argument: ". . . one thing I know, that though I was blind, now I see" (v. 25). No one could refute him.

Any time Jesus touches our lives in any way, we will be affected by both God and the world; we will receive both a crown and a cross. We will know Him as Light in our darkness, but we will also know the discomfort and loneliness of standing against a hostile world.

Our answer to the world is the same as this man's: One thing we know, that though we were blind, now we see. In the face of the sneers of the intellectuals, the questions of the critics, the threats of the vested interests, we can say what no one can refute: We know that God in Jesus Christ has touched us with life. Once we were in hopeless darkness; now we are saved by Him who is the Light of the world.

The authorities could not break the man born blind. Ridicule, insult, abuse, and pressure had been tried and had failed. They had one final weapon—excommunication.

Even when he was turned out of his faith, the man did not waver. Excommunication meant breaking with his family, his friends, his faith, his tradition, his culture—everything. But he was willing to break with them all for the sake of his loyalty to Jesus.

It is easy for us to talk about sacrifices for Christ; we make few. We live in a society permeated with the results of nineteen hundred years of Christian faith. Our loyalty to Him costs us little. We are seldom called upon to make decisive breaks with our families or friends or traditions or jobs. Christians in Asia or Africa or behind the iron or bamboo curtains have much to teach us about the cost of discipleship. The fact still remains, however, that every person who takes Jesus seriously is called upon to be willing to break with every other loyalty. In the showdown between Jesus and each of the parts of life that charm us, He demands unconditionally the first place.

Excommunication meant that this fellow was in many ways in a worse state than before he was healed; he was thrown into a new kind of darkness. Ostracized and shunned by his associates—even his family had let him down—harassed and punished by members of his religion, he must have wondered whether it had been worthwhile to obey and trust Jesus.

Jesus, however, did not abandon him. He looked for the man born blind and stood with him a second time. In our times of deepest loneliness and hopelessness, the Comforter finds us. He never gives up on us; He never deserts us.

It was during the deeper darkness of being abandoned by the world that the man born blind became completely aware who Jesus was. He learned that the depths of Jesus' concern for us more than matches the depths of our misery.

Formerly, this man had described Jesus as a Man, then as a Prophet, then as the greatest Man ever to live. It was during the blackest time of this once-blind man's life that Jesus not only came, but came revealing Himself as the God-sent Saviour. "You have seen him," Jesus assured him," and it is he who speaks to you" (v. 37). The blind beggar knew the extraordinary good news: God in person had got through to him in Jesus Christ. God could be trusted; He had brought this man from darkness to light, from death to life.

Dunkirk, France, Saturday, June 1, 1940, was a flaming inferno. One of the rescuers, an Englishman named R. B. Brett, maneuvered his small boat near the beach and jumped into the neck-high water. On the beach, a blinded soldier was standing helplessly, lost from his unit, unable to grope his way to safety, ringed with shellfire. Brett put his hand into the soldier's hand and told him to follow him. The soldier did not know Brett and he must have wondered whether it was a trap or a trick. Nevertheless, the blinded man followed Brett across the gravel and into the water. The soldier went on though the water rose to his knees, then to his hips, and finally to his armpits. He had to trust an unknown voice from someone he could not see to guide him through the perilous water and darkness. Brett stayed by the soldier. The water became neck-high. Then Brett lifted the man to his boat and safety.

Our God got down into the inferno of our world. He did not remain safely removed, a detached Spectator. God personally came into the darkness, fear, and suffering of our lives. In the life, death, and resurrection of Jesus, God reached out to forgotten, confused, hurt people. He was literally the Light of life to a beggar born blind. He is literally the same to you and He assures us that He can be trusted. He stands with us in the deep waters, the hidden terrors, and the dark loneliness of the world. He gives us His Word that He saves and heals.

Before such mercy, there is only one response. The blind man, according to John 9:38, summed it up for all of us. "He said, 'Lord, I believe'; and he worshiped him."

13

Pilate

THE NAME "Pilate" was a nickname. It meant "armed with a pike," suggesting Pilate's profession and his personality.

Tradition has it that Pilate was born in Seville, Spain. We do know that his name, Pontius, was a famous Samnite name, which would make him something of a blueblood in Roman society.

Tradition insists that Pilate had a successful army career in Europe before coming to Rome. We do know that while in Rome Pilate married Caesar Augustus' granddaughter, a refined, educated woman named Claudia Procula. Because of his marriage, Pilate found himself hobnobbing with the rulers and aristocrats.

He used his influence to get himself appointed procurator of Judea in A.D. 26. (Pilate apparently had real "pull"; he even got the rules waived so he could take Claudia with him to Judea.)

The procurator of Judea served under the governor of Judea. The procurator's job was: to keep the taxes coming in; and to keep the lid on in a troubled area. It was a tough assignment and Judea was a hotspot of political unrest.

Pilate's temperament made him a poor choice for the job. Perhaps he regarded the post as a steppingstone to bigger things; perhaps he was spoiled by his easy desk-job back in Rome. Without doubt, he was used to army ways and figured he could handle any problem as long as he had a couple of Roman legions on hand. Pilate probably missed the lights and nightlife of the capital, and must have found life in the hot, restless province hopelessly backward.

The local customs annoyed him. Making no attempt to understand the people in Judea, Pilate made the same judgment many a tourist or soldier has made in a foreign country since his time: because the people were "different," they were inferior.

Soon after Pilate arrived in Palestine, there was an uproar over the emperor's image. Wherever the Romans went, they carried the insignia of the Roman eagle with an engraving of the emperor's face. It was customary for conquered people to bow in deference whenever the emperor's standard passed.

The Jews, of course, were dead-set against allowing such an insignia inside Jerusalem because it violated the commandment against bowing before graven images. The Romans had previously respected Jewish scruples. Before entering Jerusalem, the legions had always carefully unscrewed the emperor's eagle and picture from their poles and put them away.

Not Pilate. He decided to start his term by teaching the Jews a lesson. Secretly one night, under heavy guard, he sneaked the hated insignia into Jerusalem and planted it prominently in the tower overlooking the Temple. When Jerusalem awoke next morning and found the Roman eagle in the sacred city, the population exploded with rage. Pilate could not possibly have pulled a worse blunder.

Seven thousand Jews marched on Pilate's residence in Caesarea, surrounded it, and pleaded to have the offensive image removed. Pilate merely laughed. The mob stayed and for six days and nights, every time Pilate stuck his nose outside, he saw seven thousand praying Jews.

Finally Pilate planned a trick. Sending word to the ringleaders that he would meet to discuss the matter, he secretly instructed his legionnaires to surround the area. When Pilate arrived to meet the crowd's leaders, he brusquely ordered them to tell everybody to go home quietly at once or he would give the order to have them massacred.

The leaders and the seven thousand Jews stood stock-still, daring Pilate to massacre them. Pilate had to back down. He knew he could never get away with murdering seven thousand people without word getting back to Rome. The standards and images were removed.

Next came the episode of the aqueduct. Pilate noticed that Jerusalem needed a better supply of fresh water. His problems, however, were not in engineering but financing, so he simply raided the Temple treasury. This money had been given as Temple contributions and was meant for religious purposes. When Pilate appropriated the money for his water system, fury broke out in Jerusalem.

To end the rioting, Pilate sent soldiers disguised as civilians into the crowds, against all Roman army regulations. These soldiers then used their staves on everyone, including women. In the panic, a great many were trampled or clubbed to death. When the Roman emperor Tiberius heard of this, he officially reprimanded Pilate.

As if Pilate had not learned his lesson, he triggered off still a third uproar with his arrogance. The palace of the procurator in Jerusalem was resented by the Jews. When Pilate redecorated the place with a lot of shields bearing images of heathen gods, again there was a riot.

Again, there was word from Rome: orders to remove the shields and a scathing rebuke from the emperor. This was the third time Pilate had been publicly humiliated, and it had all happened in the short space of the four years since he arrived. Pontius Pilate loathed the Jewish leaders. He worried about his own career; he had lost face too many times.

One morning at daybreak, an angry, shouting crowd of

these hated Jewish priests woke Pilate from his sleep by bursting into his courtyard and demanding to see him at once. Pilate resented the way they ordered him around. Their complaint this time? Some young Teacher they insisted should be executed immediately.

There were three parts to a Roman trial: the *accusatio* (accusation), the *interrogatio* (cross-examination), and the *excusatio* (verdict or decision). It was Pilate's responsibility to carry out civil justice.

Pilate opened the *accusatio* and asked, "What charge?" In the din, Pilate heard, "He's perverting the nation!" "He refuses to give tribute to Caesar!" "This Man claims to be a King!"

Pilate led the Prisoner inside to cross-examine Him in private. The interview that followed is carefully recorded in the gospels and remembered by generations of Christians, but Pilate probably forgot about it as one more nuisance. Jesus made it clear that He was a King, and that He had come to bear witness to the truth. Pilate's cynical comeback was the sneer, "What is truth?" (John 18:38).

Pilate knew that Jesus was innocent and deserved to be set free. When he took his place before the crowd again, he announced his verdict: "I find no crime in him" (v. 38). Suddenly, the crowd became angry and abusive. Pilate became nervous; another nasty situation was fast developing. There had been enough fuss in his term. Obviously, this Jesus was innocent, but Pilate shouted, "Then what shall I do with the man . . . ?" (Mark 15:12).

That is *the* question in life. In the following hours, Pilate tried three courses of action as answers to that all-important question.

He tried to evade the question. Having overheard that Jesus was from Galilee, Pilate remembered that Galilee was the bailiwick of Herod, a local puppet-king. Pilate figured he could duck the question by passing Jesus on to Herod.

At the same time, it would butter up Herod, with whom he had not been on friendly terms.

The case was soon back in Pilate's lap. Herod quickly lost interest in the game when Jesus refused to entertain him with some miracles. Meanwhile the crowd had grown bigger and meaner. Pilate tried another expedient. As a gesture of good will, each year at Passover time a prisoner was released. Pilate announced he would set Jesus free as a Passover concession.

The mob leaders saw this gesture for the evasion it was. They screamed for the release of a small-bore revolutionary named Barabbas. Pilate hesitated, then gave in. Barabbas was turned loose.

"What shall I do with Jesus?" Pilate was uneasy. The crowd was getting the upper hand. They knew better than Pilate that he had already evaded his duty and compromised his conscience. Pilate next tried to meet the accusers halfway. Although he knew Jesus was guiltless, Pilate decided he would satisfy the mob's lust a little bit, then set Jesus free. He called to the guards to scourge Jesus.

Scourging was a brutal form of killing a man by inches. The victim was tied to a low pole and lashed with thongs that had pieces of sharp metal embedded in the ends. A man's back was shredded to ribbons, and many victims died. A little blood, then let Jesus go, Pilate reasoned. The end justified the means.

By that time, the crowd knew instinctively that Pilate had allowed himself to be backed into a corner. He finally caved in completely. Instead of accepting personal responsibility as the procurator, he took a public-opinion poll. Although it was his job to carry out Roman justice, Pilate became an echo instead of a voice when he let the crowd make up his mind for him. Although convinced of Jesus' innocence, Pilate asked, "What shall I do with Jesus?" The answer was a deafening shriek: "*Crucify!*"

Pilate is the outstanding example of the well-adjusted man. No man was ever more in tune with others, more on the side of the majority. Pilate did the popular thing at the time—and allowed Jesus to be crucified. Note well that Pilate at no point opposed Jesus; he simply refused to take a stand.

Psychiatrists have pointed out the meaning of the little tableau that Pilate went through with the basin and the towel. He publicly and dramatically claimed he was washing his hands of the whole mess—something only a man with a deep sense of guilt would do. Pilate tried to transfer responsibility to the crowd. Interestingly, Jesus the night before had also called for a basin and a towel. Pilate washed his own hands, refusing to become involved or to take a stand; Jesus washed the disciples' feet, choosing to become involved and to take a stand. One name is remembered with disgust, the Other with reverence.

"What shall I do with Jesus?" This is also your question. You can try to evade it. "Give me time to think it over. Let me resolve all my doubts first. Let me wait until all the evidence is in. Wait until I get a chance to do some more reading." But the question still burns because it is Question Number One in everyone's life.

You can try to compromise. You can try to tell yourself, "Oh, it's all right as long as my heart is in the right place." Pilate's heart was in the right place, too. But that was not enough. He wouldn't lift a finger to carry out his feelings. His convictions were never translated into action. He simply did what was expedient: he allowed Jesus to be executed.

You may say your intentions are good, but are you roused to do anything about those intentions? How about even the most casual responsibilities of doing something with Jesus? Are you worshiping regularly and joining in the church's ministry, or have you compromised? Do you systematically share a proportion of your income, or is it expedient not to? Are you witnessing as a Christian at work, or is it easier to keep quiet? Decent impulses are never enough. "What shall I do with Jesus?" demands your obedience.

You can try to shift the responsibility. "Why doesn't 'someone' do something about such-and-such?" you demand. "Why don't 'they' take care of that at the church?" The question is still, "What shall *I* do with Jesus," not "What will somebody do with Jesus?"

Pilate didn't want to stick his neck out or be a nonconformist. Nobody likes conflict or unpopularity. We want to "fit in," especially when it's with a group that has a lot to do with our ambitions, our careers, and our pocketbooks. We try to be amiable, agreeable folks who know how to get along with people. Like Pilate, we try to transfer responsibility for Jesus to the crowd.

"What shall I do with Jesus?" Ultimately, there are only two answers. Either "Crucify Him!" or "Lord, have mercy upon me a sinner." Evasion, compromise, and transfer of responsibility add up to allowing Him to be crucified. In other words, you take a stand for Jesus or against Him—you can have it only one way or the other.

Pilate lasted only a few more years in Judea. His interview with Jesus apparently made little difference to his fading career and he was ordered to Rome after butchering a large number of Samaritans in a minor disturbance near Mt. Gerizim. The historian Eusebius recounts the legend that after Pontius Pilate was recalled to Rome, he was exiled to Gaul and later given instructions to carry out his own execution. He took his own life and his body was cast into the Rhone River. Legend has it that the waters were so disturbed at receiving Pilate's body that the corpse was pushed north to Lake Lucerne to the foot of the large mountain now called Mt. Pilatus. Medieval tales tell of his body rising from the lake on Good Friday to sit on the shore, washing its hands, or bobbing to the surface when its name is spoken and begging for sympathy with staring eyes.

Actually, Pilate comes to rest in every city in the world. He may be found in any place where you and I refuse to stand with Jesus.

"What shall I do with Jesus?" What *can* we do but accept Him, trust Him, and obey Him?

14

The Two Thieves

THE MEN called him "Mousey" or "the Mouse." He was short, sharp-faced, and had a streak of rodentlike meanness in him. Nobody ever caught him, but everybody suspected that Mousey picked up things like shaving cream belonging to the other G.I.'s. A couple of times, cartons of cigarettes were missed, and all the evidence pointed to the Mouse.

Mousey did nothing to endear himself to the others. He whined constantly, shirked his duties in his company. Always borrowing something, he had never been known to return anything. He even broke the unwritten law of the unit by tattling to the lieutenant about a couple of his buddies.

The outfit was shipped to the Pacific. It was assigned to hit one of those forgotten pinpoints on the map, a tiny protrusion of Japanese-held coral that had to be bought with lots of American blood.

The action was over by late afternoon. The medics looked for American wounded among the bodies around the smoking bunkers, and they found Mousey, still conscious. All they could do for him, however, was to give him a hefty shot of morphine and move on to the next man.

A chaplain bent over the Mouse and tried to comfort him. Mousey whispered something. The chaplain bent over the dying boy to catch what he was saying. The Mouse gasped, "Can I—*can I*—be forgiven?"

Some people may brush aside this incident as not being a true example of Christian repentance. "Deathbed conversion!" others sneer. Still others treat the question as merely an evening's topic to discuss.

Mousey's question still stands. Unless we can answer with a positive yes or no, we do not have a faith fit or relevant for Mousey or anyone.

Three men shared death on a hill one afternoon. All three hung on crosses. All three passed through the valley of the shadow of death.

Two of the doomed were "thieves." Perhaps they were literally purse-snatchers, thugs, part of the hordes of half-savage desert men who infested the wild areas such as the Jericho road, brutally beating and robbing travelers. Perhaps these two were part of that fringe of society we call "criminal," warped and stunted people who can unblinkingly gang up on a victim for "kicks" or a few coins.

The word for "thief" in Greek is also used for "revolutionary." Possibly the two on crosses beside Jesus were plotters, members of one of the dozens of clandestine Palestinian groups organized to throw out the Romans. Perhaps they had moved in a shadowy world of terror, intrigue, and violence, living on the dreams of a future that was to follow their revolution.

In any case, they were winding up their lives in total dishonor. Not even an electric chair today carries the stigma of disgrace that a cross did then. These two thieves had been hunted down and were being exterminated as beasts of prey. Society had totally rejected them, casting them out by the most disparaging symbol it had—crucifixion.

It is peculiarly significant that Jesus also died in this way. God identified Himself with the despised and rejected. Our God was not dignified or proud. He took the horselaughs and jeers, the reproach and disgrace of a cross.

How like Jesus to spend His last hours with two unwanted

thieves and not with His disciples or in the company of friends in the home at Bethany. He died as He had lived, among society's rejects.

Were the two thieves young men? If so, they probably thought to themselves that they had not done very much in life; there were so many dreams unfulfilled. Perhaps the thought slipped through their minds that they had followed the wrong dreams. Or, were they older men? If so, they would have looked back on wasted years. Perhaps they recalled how time had sneaked by until now it was too late, too late. Old or young, these men had nothing but squandered lives.

Crucifixions, like any public cruelty, brought out all that was not-so-pretty in people. The bystanders were a rough crowd, shouting wisecracks and tormenting the victims. Some of the more cruel of the wits thought they were in better form than usual. Enraged, the two thieves snarled and shrieked epithets.

Jesus, however, suffered in silence; this made Him bigger game for the loudmouths in the mob. ". . . come down now from the cross," one tormentor yelled, "that we may see and believe" (Mark 15:32). The taunts grew louder as the crowd learned that the silent Victim was Jesus. Even the two thieves cursed Him and joined in the jeers. Jesus did not growl back at them nor hurl hate at the mocking crowd. Unlike other crucified men, Jesus did not scream for vengeance, swear over His misfortune, or answer those insulting Him.

Dimly, the thieves became aware that the Man on the third cross was different. His quiet dignity set Him apart. Both thieves spoke to Jesus in their last moments: one thief sneered; the other worshiped.

Bitterly, the first thief demanded that Jesus save him. This man was so shot through with selfishness that even the other thief was stunned and bawled him out: "Do you not fear

God, since you are under the same sentence of condemnation? And we indeed justly; for we are receiving the due reward of our deeds; but this man has done nothing wrong" (Luke 23:40-41).

The second thief was willing to be honest where it was hardest—about himself. Hanging beside that silent Fellow Sufferer, the second thief noted that Jesus had asked for no favors or relief for Himself. Knowing what a contrast Jesus' life and dying was to his, this thief gave up the deceit he had been practicing about himself before the world and before God. He even had the courage to tell his buddy, the first thief, to face up to himself. They were both sinners and it was high time they admitted it.

Jesus was able to inspire confidence in Himself, even in His dying moments. A hardened criminal, a hunted and hated member of the underworld, came clean before Jesus.

Not even the disciples called Jesus by His first name, but always addressed Him as "Rabbi" or "Teacher." This thief called Him "Jesus" to His face. He obviously felt Jesus was his Friend. A piece of unwanted human scum was made to feel an intimacy with Jesus. The thief asked in effect, "Can I—*can I*—be forgiven?"

Mousey's question was asked—and answered—nineteen hundred years ago on a hill outside Jerusalem. Jesus spoke an overwhelming "Yes." ". . . today," He said to a man who had sinned away his life, "you will be with me in Paradise" (Luke 23:43).

The crucified Jesus who inspired a first-name relationship with a dying thief also inspired a confidence in Himself as God. Because of Jesus, that thief—and Mousey, and you and I—can be on first-name terms with God!

Suppose any of us had been in that situation? We might have put the thief in his place for having jeered at us earlier. Or we might have told him to shut up and let us die in peace. "Can't you see that I have enough problems of my own?"

would have been our retort. Or, assuming we could have mustered enough patience for a civil answer, we would have had to tell the thief, "Sorry; I'm in the same boat as you. I'm as helpless and ignorant as the next guy in a fix like this."

The famous Swiss theologian Karl Barth regularly preaches at the city jail in Basel. In one of his sermons there, he describes this scene of Jesus and the two thieves as "the first certain Christian community." Here for the first time the promise is heard and believed.

The promise of God's forgiveness is present this day. "*Today* you will be with me in paradise." God's mercy in Jesus Christ is not "sometime." That old song "In the Sweet Bye and Bye" may be a catchy foot-thumper, but the words never quite say anything. Jesus promises His presence in the not-so-sweet present. Reconciliation with God is not in a vague future, or after we die.

In January, 1960, an astounding event occurred in a tiny peasant village of Tsirkuny in the Ukraine. A smelly, sunken-jawed wretch named Grisha Sikalenko appeared one morning before his shocked neighbors. Everyone thought that Grisha had died a hero's death while fighting the Germans in World War II. Actually, the night Grisha marched away to war, he had deserted and sneaked home. His mother made a hiding place for him under the manure pile at the back of the goatshed and for eighteen years Grisha had existed in a living grave. Twice a day his mother sneaked food to him. In winters, he nearly froze; in summers, nearly suffocated. Year after year, he lived out his miserable existence in the reeking pit, throwing away his life, afraid to face up to the punishment for desertion.

Finally, Grisha came out of hiding, expecting to be prosecuted and horribly punished. His fears were groundless. The statute of limitations had long since made him immune from prosecution.

Many of us huddle in our self-made prisons, often for years, often for a lifetime. We try to exist in the misery of pits of selfishness. Foolishly afraid of God, we shrink from Him, thinking He will punish us.

The cross destroys that fear. On the cross, God reaches out to us, offering us forgiveness now. In Jesus Christ, God assures us that we can leave our self-imposed prisons. We are forgiven—*now*. Like the thief, we are meant to know the immediacy, the *now*-ness, the *today*-ness of Christ's transforming friendship.

God's forgiveness in Jesus is also private. "Today *you* will be with me. . . ." God welcomes anyone, even individual thieves and outcasts.

In this day we think of people in the mass. We speak of people as fractions of some huge, impersonal mass—a department, a crew, a section, a battalion, a congregation, a shift. We become merely one of many "hands" at a plant. Modern industrial society forgets that each person is separate, a distinct individual, a walking portfolio of problems, fears, dreams, heartaches, burnt-out hopes, and unfinished business. In crowded cities and as parts of organizations, we forget others. But God does not forget. "Today *you*," He says, "will be with me." No man or woman is a coded index-card with God. The cross is His hand-written invitation to you to come and live.

If you want to be critical, this thief's prayer was poorly worded. It was selfish: ". . . remember me . . ." (Luke 23:42). We can find lots wrong with the phrasing. However, it was the outpouring of a man in desperate need for forgiveness—and that was all that was necessary! Admitting he needed God's help, he asked for Him and he trusted Him.

We do not have to use the "church-y" words. We do not have to fit into the stereotype of the "religious" person. God looks within us to see how honest we are in asking for help.

At the cross God saw a man praying selfishly, yet admitting he was at the end of his own resources. He answered that man.

God welcomes anyone—even a thief like that man, even a minister like me, even a housewife or salesman like you, even a deadbeat like Mousey.

God's forgiveness is personal. The dying thief knew that God was there beside him, accepting him. God was there in that Partner on the other cross. No flimsy hope or cheap comfort from Jesus! He gave the thief a direct promise, a promise without secret clauses or fine print.

When a man gets to his lowest ebb and turns to the Christ who is ever near, he finds that Jesus sticks by His word. The cross stands for the personal concern of the personal God.

One of the unanswered questions perpetually haunting human beings is, What is it like after we die? Sooner or later in every discussion on faith, the subject pops up. A few years ago, nonsense swept the country about an Irish woman named Bridey Murphy who was said to have been "reincarnated" when a Denver housewife was under a hypnotic trance. In addition to showing how gullible the American public is, it also showed how desperate we are for some assurance that a coffin and six feet of dirt are not the last words. Some of the people who swallowed the Bridey Murphy hoax obviously believed it because they wanted to believe in *something*, and grabbed at any straw.

The last word is not from the fakery and mumbo-jumbo of a hypnotized woman with an overcharged imagination. The final word is still from the God-sent Man on the cross: ". . . you will be with me. . . ." That sums up everything we need to know. With Him! What more can anyone ask?

"Today, you will be with me in paradise." There are only three ways of taking these words: (1) Jesus was lying, deliberately deceiving that dying thief; (2) Jesus was terribly mistaken; (3) Jesus was correct.

Lying, perhaps? But Jesus consistently stuck to the truth. He could have dodged the cross, but He was so uncompromising in His personal integrity and so unswerving in His devotion to truth that He laid down His life. A lie to that thief would be completely out of character. Further, it would have been the only instance of Jesus ever stating a falsehood. We can rule out a lie by Jesus.

Then, perhaps, mistaken? Not by a longshot! God raised up the Christ they had crucified; He was seen alive. Jesus was vindicated.

Jesus was correct. He could hold out the offer of life to a thief.

Three men shared death on a hill that afternoon. All three hung on crosses. All three passed through the valley of the shadow. But only one man died. The other two—the penitent thief and Jesus—made a rendezvous.

15

Mary Magdalene and Thomas

ABOUT EIGHT hundred years ago, Valencia was besieged by the Moors. For a long time, the small Spanish garrison withstood the assaults of the Moors because of the inspired leadership of a hero named Ruy Diaz de Bivar, usually called el Cid. The time finally came when el Cid died of old age and battle fatigue. His lieutenants, however, dressed his body in armor, tied his sword in his right hand, and by a cleverly-made wicker framework which was carefully concealed, they propped the corpse on his horse. With the mounted cadaver leading the column, the Spanish forces charged out the gates of Valencia.

Some critics of the church claim that Easter is much the same thing. They claim that the early disciples of Jesus wanted to perpetuate the great man's life, so they announced that He was not really dead at all. These critics state that His followers simply made a brave and noble attempt to rally around the memory of Jesus.

Is this what the resurrection amounts to? Were the disciples simply "propping up" Jesus, trying to make Him appear real? Were these followers simply a group of die-hards who refused to admit they were licked, and made one last supreme effort to convince themselves and others that they were not? Were they simpletons trying to kid themselves into thinking Jesus was still with them?

Is Easter merely an occasion when we pay our respects to

a clever hoax? Do we gather each Sunday morning simply to prop up the memory of a long-dead Teacher?

When the Spaniards galloped out of Valencia behind the corpse of el Cid on horseback, they were quickly defeated. Their hearts were not in the battle. The dead body of their leader could not inspire them; neither did it fool the enemy.

Do not put Easter in the same category as the hoax of Valencia. The resurrection of Jesus Christ was not a bold trick carefully plotted by His followers. Even a hurried reading of the gospel accounts will show that none of them expected Jesus to be seen alive again. Further, no hoax can inspire those who are parties to it. The men of Valencia failed, partly because they were in on the piece of fakery. The followers of Jesus were strengthened and enthused, and no hoax could have done that. Instead of collapsing, as frauds eventually must, the Good News of the resurrection gained momentum and has been the pivotal announcement of all recorded history.

Is there evidence that the resurrection was not a clever effort to perpetuate Jesus' memory? Look at two of those who were present: Mary Magdalene and Thomas. Mary Magdalene was the first to see the risen Lord; Thomas was the first to doubt that the Lord had been raised. These two, the first witness and the first skeptic, deserve careful study.

Both Mary Magdalene and Thomas were unlikely followers of Jesus. "Magdalene" means that Mary hailed from the village of Magdala, a notorious red-light district of Galilee. It was corrupt, rich, and tough, and anybody from Magdala usually had a dubious reputation. There is little doubt about Mary of Magdala. The New Testament mentions that she had had seven demons cast out by Jesus. In Jewish wording in those days, immorality was described as "demon-possession." Sevenfold demon-possession meant complete abandonment to shame. In other words, Mary

Magdalene had been a prostitute. Once a depraved, hardened cynic, she had allowed herself to be passed from man to man like a dirty magazine, seized eagerly, used briefly, then thrown aside. She had been plucked from a life of futility and guilt by Jesus.

Thomas was also an unlikely disciple. Although he was not tagged with a sordid past like Mary Magdalene, Thomas by nature was a stubborn individualist, a no-nonsense realist. For example, at the Last Supper, Jesus spoke, "In my Father's house are many mansions. . . . I go to prepare a place for you. And if I go . . . , I will come again, and receive you unto myself; that where I am, there ye may be also. And whither I go ye know, and the way ye know" (John 14:2-4, KJV).

Blunt-spoken Thomas did not understand. "Lord, we know not whither thou goest; and how can we know the way?" he said (v. 5). This was a man who did not hesitate to interrupt when he was puzzled. No easily excited enthusiast, Thomas was the original "man from Missouri," a cautious, deliberate, factual man.

Both Mary Magdalene and Thomas were unexpecting witnesses of the risen Jesus. Neither they, nor any other disciple, had the faintest glimmer of hope of ever seeing Jesus alive after the crucifixion. They knew the grisly details of a death on a cross: the sickening sight of a twitching human body, the gruesome sounds of a man breathing his last, the flies, the stench, the blood. No one survived that. Jesus' life, they knew, was stamped "Case Closed."

Mary Magdalene waited until the Jewish sabbath was over, then crept through the predawn darkness to the tomb where Jesus' body had been laid. It was customary at that time for women to perform the few simple chores of preparing a body for burial by placing spices next to the corpse. Mary Magdalene had gathered a supply of spices and was on her way to prepare Jesus' body for burial. Obviously, she was not expecting to find anything except a lifeless, mutilated corpse. The principal thought in her mind that morning was the problem of getting the stone pushed aside so that she could get into the tomb. Tombs were chambers hewn from the soft limestone found everywhere near Jerusalem. The entrances usually were about three feet square and were sealed by a rock slab. Sometimes the slab-door was round so that it could be rolled aside; sometimes it was square. In any case, it was a heavy, cumbersome thing to shift. Mary Magdalene was concerned that she would not be able to move the stone herself. She obviously was not expecting the resurrection.

When she came to the tomb, to her dismay she found it empty. Mary did not think that anything significant had happened. The empty tomb at first meant to her that somebody had moved Jesus' body. It was one more cruel trick on the part of the authorities, or somebody, one more problem for Mary Magdalene. She would have to locate someone for information, then pick up the heavy burden of spices and search out the new location of the corpse.

Mary Magdalene reacted in a very human way: she broke down and cried. The arrest and trial of Jesus, the torture, the walk to Calvary, the crucifixion—all these had taken everything out of Mary Magdalene. The last thing on her mind was any thought of Jesus being raised.

"Woman, why are you weeping?" a voice asked (John 20:15).

Why was she weeping? Why does anyone weep when a loved one dies? Mary Magdalene cried as any of us cry when we realize that death means complete and permanent separation from the person we must bury. She was also weeping from regret. She was disappointed with the makeshift burial. Perhaps she was berating herself for not staying around to see that Jesus' body was not moved.

Her tears, however, were more than an expression of

grief and regret. Mary Magdalene was bitter. Life was a dirty joke, a cruel mistake. Perhaps she remembered her life back in Magdala, and how Jesus had given her the awareness that God cared and could be trusted. The horrible death of Jesus, the one good Man in the world, only brought Mary back to her old way of thinking that everything was stupid and senseless. She had come out to pay her respects to His dead body and she could not even do that. God? Where was He? God was helpless. God had been outmaneuvered, defeated, outsmarted, and stopped by men of power and cruelty. When they hounded Jesus and hung Him on a cross, they really showed how helpless God is. When the chips are down, Mary told herself, a person is alone and deserted.

This is what we too so often think. "Why are you weeping?" the voice persists. This is the voice of the risen Jesus Christ. This is the God who will not be stopped by death, the God who addresses us still.

What stops us does not stop God. We put God to the test; we challenged Him by taking away Jesus' earthly survival. We rate self-preservation as the most vital and important thing, and we took *this* away from Jesus Christ. We flung the glove across God's face and challenged Him to do something about a cross.

God took up the challenge and raised up Jesus Christ from the dead. Once and for all, God demonstrated that He is in absolute control. He cannot and will not be defeated. "Why are you weeping?" He asks. In effect He says, "Have you forgotten that I am even stronger than death itself, that not even the powers of decay and destruction can hold Me?"

In the risen Christ, God affirms that He sticks by His creation. He does not write us off; rather, as Creator, He completes what He began. Creation was not a mistake and life is not a dirty joke. "Why are you weeping?" He inquires. "I mean to stay with you and with My world. Nothing—not even death—will stop Me. I will reach down to where there are no possibilities, to the grave itself, and resurrect you as I have resurrected Jesus Christ."

Mary Magdalene was addressed by the risen, living Jesus. She was confronted by One who asked her why she was weeping. This was not God playing at charades, or acting out a little doctrine. In that Man alive, God confronted her with life.

Mary still did not respond. She was sniffling about life's sadness. In spite of the voice and the presence of the risen Jesus beside her, she was too caught up in her tears and troubles, and assumed that the Person speaking to her was a cemetery gardener or handyman.

"Mary," the voice said, calling her by name (v. 16). The risen Christ spoke to her personally, as a Friend. The resurrection was first known by a sobbing woman who had come to carry out the funeral chores and was called by name by the risen Lord. God did not announce this news to the masses from the Temple square in Jerusalem, or through an edict or dramatic revelation to Pilate, Caiaphas, or the emperor in Rome. He simply appeared to Mary Magdalene, quietly calling her by her own name. There was no thundering, impersonal voice bellowing, "You there by the tomb!" He simply said, "Mary."

We often approach the Christian faith as if we were going to look idly at the story of a tomb. We often limp through Lent each year, expecting only to memorialize a corpse. We are meant to know that Jesus Christ lives. He calls each of us by name.

We live in an impersonal world which takes away our names and makes us into a faceless series of digits. We are numbers to the Social Security office, the bank, the corporation, the insurance company. We enter life as Maternity

Case Number Such-and-Such, and end life simply as an event in Parlor B of a funeral home, in a casket with a coded description and decorations, Class II.

God in the resurrection of Jesus Christ corrects that painful delusion. He assures us that we are not mere numbers but beloved children, with an eternal place in His mind and love.

Mary Magdalene, electrified by the Good News of the resurrection, raced to tell it to the Twelve. They refused to take her seriously; her story sounded too improbable. They, too, were obviously not expecting Jesus to be raised. In fact, the disciples were huddled behind barricaded doors, shivering with fright. Disillusioned and despondent, they were uncertain about their plans, afraid to be seen on the streets. Two of their number sneaked out of town to return to the safety of their homes in Galilee.

During the next few days, however, Jesus appeared personally to clusters of His followers. Mary Magdalene's report was not "an idle tale" (Luke 24:11), as they had called it, but the most stupendous news they could imagine. Jesus was alive!

For some reason, Thomas had not been with the other disciples when Jesus had appeared to them after the crucifixion. Thomas, of course, quickly heard about these appearances of the risen Jesus, but he would not allow himself to be swept off his feet by fantastic reports. Jesus had been killed; He was dead, stone-cold dead; dead men do not rise up. Others might be carried away with the announcement that Jesus was raised up alive, but not Thomas. The others pressed him to believe them but Thomas was determined. Bluntly, he told them that he would have to be shown. Until he personally poked his fingers into the nail holes and the gaping wound in Jesus' side, he did not want to hear any more. If his conditions were met, if he got to probe the wounds with his own hands, then he would believe.

Thomas was the original show-me type of believer. He couldn't accept the claims of others, even though they were his good friends. He had to have his own personal evidence, something he could see and feel himself.

Perhaps this is the kind of believer you are: disillusioned, questioning, confused. Perhaps you are even a member of the church, but you tell yourself that you cannot buy the church's "party line." It is too pat, too neat. You may even be secretly rebellious at having to go along with the crowd —even the church crowd. Just because everybody else is there, and just because everybody else says so, does not mean it is true, you may feel. It's not that you're trying to be an obnoxious nonconformist; it's simply that you feel left out. You have questions about the goodness and presence of God. You are not a wise-guy atheist; you left that role behind when you left the sophomore class. But you would like some inkling, some sign from God. It would help to clinch things in your mind.

Perhaps, like Thomas, you have even set up little tests. "If God is around, as everybody says He is, let Him do thus-and-so. Then I'll believe," you tell Him.

At times, we all act like cunning employers setting up clever traps to check up on employees about whom we're uneasy. So you and I insist we must test God to find out if He is still on the job. If He meets the test, fine; God is great and we'll believe. If not, well, our suspicions were correct in the first place.

Thomas set up his own tests to determine whether Jesus had been raised from the dead. If the lab results were positive, if he got to touch the wounds and scars in Jesus, then Thomas would believe in the resurrection.

But nothing happened. A day passed. Then two days, three, four, five came and went. A week elapsed, and still there was no "sign" or "proof" for Thomas. No sign; therefore, no resurrection, Thomas was undoubtedly thinking.

Skeptical Thomas, however, did something that doubting moderns seldom do. Even though he was not at first convinced of the resurrection, he maintained his loyalty to Jesus. He had little hope, but he had a gritty determination to keep going along the lines he once had with Jesus. Even though he had only the memory of a dead Jesus to cling to, he was loyal to that memory.

Then one day, quietly and undramatically, Jesus appeared again to the disciples. This time, Thomas was present. Going deliberately to Thomas, Jesus showed him His hands and side and told him to reach out and touch them for himself. Gasped Thomas, "My Lord and my God!" (John 20:28).

Thomas' unbelief gave way to belief, not by the removal of his intellectual difficulties but by his awareness of the goodness of God in the risen Jesus. The mercy and presence of God through the mighty act of the resurrection conquered Thomas, not "answers" and "proofs." Thomas learned that he did not have to carry out his tests in order to believe. Even though they were all fulfilled, they were really not necessary. Thomas saw that God wants to renew fellowship with lost, lonely men and women. The resurrection of Jesus Christ was this Good News.

In coming to Thomas, the risen Christ also came to you and me. He is not interested in playing an intellectual game of hide-and-seek, asking us to guess where He hid. He comes to us as His children, not as challenges.

We can forget about any tests we have put up for God, or the proofs we have demanded. God is much more concerned about you and me than He is about our silly little tests and proofs.

If you have been trying God out, if you have been checking Him out, forget it. This has been done once and for all time, for you and for all men. In coming to Thomas, God in Christ brushed aside your conditions for believing as well as Thomas'. The living Lord has come, seeking, accepting, and saving you personally. In coming to Thomas, He came to every tired, cynical doubter.

Unfortunately, the church has often given the impression that the doubter is condemned. Sadly, history is full of unpleasant occasions where the church has implied that the doubter is a hopeless sinner who does not belong in its fellowship, and is completely cut off from God. Whenever the church has condemned the doubter, it has failed her Lord. When He came to Thomas, He in effect came to you and me, to all who are disillusioned, to all who doubt. He tells us that we are not cut off from God but that we belong to Him. In spite of our confusion and uncertainty, He accepts you and me.

Is the resurrection a hoax? Is Easter an attempt to prop up a dead hero? Hardly, when you investigate the personal experiences of those present, especially those who found it hardest to believe.

Thomas spoke for all believers and for all time when he exclaimed before the risen Christ, "My Lord and my God!" This is the only response anyone can make to the claim that Jesus lives. Mary Magdalene spoke for all believers and for all time when she witnessed before the world, "I have seen the Lord . . ." (John 20:18). Ultimately, this is the only response we who have been touched with life can make.

Related Scripture Passages

MARY, THE MOTHER OF JESUS

Matthew 1:18-25 12:46-50; 13:53-58; Luke 2; John 2:1-12; 19:25-27; Acts 1:14.

PHILIP

Matthew 10:3; Mark 3:14-19; John 1:43-51; 6:5-14; 12:20-22; 14:1-12; Acts 1:13.

ANDREW

Matthew 4:18-20; 10:2; Mark 13:3; John 1:35-42; 6:5-14; 12:20-22; Acts 1:13.

NICODEMUS

John 3:1-21; 7:40-52; 19:38-42.

ZACCHAEUS

Luke 19:1-10.

THE RICH YOUNG RULER

Matthew 19:16-26; Mark 10:17-27; Luke 18:18-30.

THE WOMAN OF SAMARIA

John 4:1-42.

PETER, JAMES, AND JOHN

Matthew 4:18-22; 17:1-13; Mark 3:16-17; 14:32-42; Luke 8:49-56; Acts 4:13; 12:1-3.

THE GADARENE DEMONIAC

Matthew 8:28-34; Mark 5:1-20; Luke 8:26-40.

SIMON THE PHARISEE AND THE REPENTANT WOMAN

Luke 7:36-50.

MARY, MARTHA, AND LAZARUS

Luke 10:38-42; John 11:1-12:11.

THE MAN BORN BLIND

John 9:1-41.

PILATE

Matthew 27:1-26; John 18:28-19:22.

THE TWO THIEVES

Matthew 27:38-44; Luke 23:32-43.

MARY MAGDALENE AND THOMAS

John 14: 1-7; 20:1-29.

Index to Names

Index to Scriptures

OLD TESTAMENT

NEW TESTAMENT